Osvaldo César Ardiles was born in Córdoba in 1952 and played a pivotal role in Argentina's World Cup victory in 1978, part of 63 caps he won for his country. That famous ticker-tape win in Buenos Aires attracted the attention of Tottenham Hotspur manager Keith Burkinshaw, who brought Ossie and Ricardo Villa over to England in a £750,000 transfer that made headlines around the world.

Ossie became an instant hit in English football, helping Spurs lift the FA Cup in 1981 and 1982 and the UEFA Cup in 1984 and going on to score 25 goals in 311 appearances during ten years at the club. Ossie moved into management with Swindon Town and took them into the top flight of English football for the first time, only to have promotion snatched away owing to irregular payments made to players before Ardiles' arrival at the club. Further managerial spells followed at Newcastle, West Brom (with whom he also won promotion) and then back at Tottenham, where, despite an exhilarating attacking line-up, results did not go Ossie's way.

Ossie has since managed clubs in Mexico, Japan, Croatia, Saudi Arabia, Argentina, Israel and Paraguay. He has lived in Hertfordshire since making England his home.

Marcela Mora y Araujo is an Argentinian football writer and broadcaster. She was the translator of Diego Maradona's autobiography *El Diego* and co-editor of two volumes of football literature anthologies, *Perfect Pitch*. She lives in London.

Ossie's Dream:

The Autobiography
of a Football Legend

Ossie Ardiles

with Marcela Mora y Araujo

CORGI BOOKS

TRANSWORLD PUBLISHERS
61–63 Uxbridge Road, London W5 5SA
A Random House Group Company
www.rbooks.co.uk

OSSIE'S DREAM
A CORGI BOOK: 9780552159180

First published in Great Britain
in 2009 by Bantam Press
an imprint of Transworld Publishers
Corgi edition published 2010

Addresses for Random House Group Ltd companies outside the UK
can be found at: www.randomhouse.co.uk
The Random House Group Ltd Reg. No. 954009

The Random House Group Limited supports The Forest Stewardship Council
(FSC), the leading international forest certification organisation. All our titles that
are printed on Greenpeace approved FSC certified paper carry the FSC logo. Our
paper procurement policy can be found at
www.rbooks.co.uk/environment

Typeset in 12/17pt Minion by
Falcon Oast Graphic Art Ltd.
Printed in the UK by CPI Cox & Wyman, Reading, RG1 8EX.

2 4 6 8 10 9 7 5 3 1

Mixed Sources
Product group from well-managed
forests and other controlled sources
www.fsc.org Cert no. TT-COC-2139
© 1996 Forest Stewardship Council
FSC

To Silvia,
To my mother Blanca,
and to my grandchildren Sofia and the twins,
Benjamin and Sebastian

Contents

Prologue

It's funny how, looking back, one can clearly see a moment that changes everything. Just a few seconds, and my life could have turned out to be completely different.

There I was, coming out from way, way at the back, and the Peruvian midfielder Teófilo Cubillas, undoubtedly one of the great players of his generation, comes up to me and really puts the pressure on. And I dummied him ever so slightly and managed to nutmeg the ball through his legs, recover it and keep it for our side. It was a huge risk because I was the last man and had he pinched it off me he might have scored – and if he had done, I wouldn't have played in the World Cup.

I wouldn't have played in the World Cup, I wouldn't have won the World Cup, and I almost certainly wouldn't have come to England. My whole life would have been completely different.

But I pulled it off, a nutmeg against one of the legends of my time. A nutmeg! In Argentina that's the kind of thing the fans love. I had done thousands in my time, it wasn't a special one, but it was a crowd-pleasing move, and it came at a crucial time. From then on, I noticed nobody questioned me any more. My confidence went sky-high again and I stayed in the squad, played and won the World Cup, moved to Tottenham.

So one moment in time can change a whole life.

1

La Nuestra

There's something about the Argentinian mentality that brags about being the best at everything. In football, too, of course, we had this idea that we were the best. But results didn't back that up. In the 1974 World Cup Argentina were humiliated. After that César Luis Menotti took over and instituted a completely different philosophy. I wouldn't say a revolution because that's a very dramatic word and I don't go for drama in that way; I don't like to use such drastic terms. But I think without a doubt that the modern era in Argentinian football began when César took over the national squad.

The type of football that had prevailed in Argentina was exemplified by Estudiantes de la Plata, who achieved unprecedented success in terms of trophies and international competitions but who worked to an ethic that pushed the rule book to the limit. Known as 'the anti-football', it was regarded at worst as dirty and at best as extremely competitive, in the sense that everything was fair and valid as long as victory was achieved. Everything, including verbal abuse, even insulting your opponent's mother – the psychological denigration of the opponent. Estudiantes' football was about stretching the rules to breaking point, the idea being to bother your rival as much as possible – a fact to which the Manchester United side of 1968, which met Estudiantes in the World Club Cup Final that year, could give testimony.

César's philosophy was totally opposite to that. It basically said, 'We're going to play well, we're going to play our way, *la nuestra.*' *La nuestra* is all about touch and keeping possession – it's beautiful football. In short, it is also my philosophy of football.

With the national team we were a bit more direct, in the sense that when our opponents had the ball and started playing we would put a lot more pressure on them. We didn't ease off, we didn't back off, we didn't back down, and then when we won the ball back our first thought was to counter-attack quickly, if we could. If not, pass, so that we retained possession, while probing for an opening.

César liked to win the ball as quickly as possible. His

thinking – and mine, I would say – was that when you don't have the ball, make life as difficult as possible for the other team. When the other side has the ball the main thing is to recover it as soon as possible, by playing, as we say, *al achique*. I guess that means pressing, but pressing in a way that reduces the size of the pitch – I mean, making the playing area as small as you can: when you have the ball, try to open up the pitch as much as possible; when your opponents have it, close down the pitch as much as possible. Playing the way, for example, Holland did in 1974 – one of the best teams I've seen in my life.

The basic philosophy behind possession football is that if your team succeeds in always having the ball, touching and passing it around, soon the other team becomes desperate for possession. But for it to work you need good players, intelligent players. I've seen many as a player and even more as a manager. I can see the qualities from the outside but they're not so easy to transmit to players. It's one thing being a good juggler of the ball, quite another to be a good player. Being a good player is about knowing how to make decisions: each ball you play must be pure intelligence.

You may have seen players who rarely touch the ball. It's as if they go one way and the ball goes another. How can this be? It happens because they don't understand the game. In the 1978 Argentina squad we had a lot of players who really understood the game, in every position – defence, midfield and attack. A player like Luis Galván, for example. He was very small, and rather limited technically, but he knew when to go left, when to go right, when just to lean towards the right, when to go out, when to stay put . . . Excellent timing is so important for a defender.

César didn't say much to us in terms of what to do. He never said to me 'go down the left', 'go down the right' or anything like that. Of course he warned us to watch out for certain players, for example, but that was about as far as his instructions went. He did talk a lot about football, but not just about football: he did not impart specific instructions so much as lyrical reflections on his playing philosophy.

As I said, it was a radical change from the essentially mean, nasty anti-football Argentina were accustomed to. Estudiantes was the club that won everything, even the World Club Cup, and other clubs followed Estudiantes. But not River Plate. Their manager simply chose the ones who played best and let them get out there and play. There were some terrific players at River at the time – the likes of Norberto Alonso, Daniel Passarella and J. J. López – and they played some very beautiful football. That team played very well, without a doubt. But the competitive element in Argentinian football was still so overwhelming, as long as you could get the rival off your back, everything and anything was allowed. Was it dirty? Of course, but also at the national level we didn't win anything. César changed all that.

He was appointed manager of Argentina in December 1974. At the time I was already established as one of the top players of what we call 'the interior' of Argentina (in Argentina, everywhere that isn't Buenos Aires is 'the interior'). In 1975 I was transferred to Huracán, a Buenos Aires club which was by common consent one of the top clubs in the country then. The only team that could compete against Huracán was Boca, though we were clearly the better side. I had already played for a provincial squad from the interior which existed then, a prestigious call-up that was one step below the national squad, though we played internationally as well. Menotti had picked me for the provincial squad, so once I was at Huracán there was a strong possibility I would make it into the national squad.

The following year, 1976, five of us from Huracán – Héctor Baley, René Houseman, Omar Larrosa, Jorge Carrascosa and me – were picked for Menotti's initial squad list for a tour of Europe. As well as the change in approach on the pitch, one of the very significant things that tour achieved was that it overcame a huge inferiority complex we Argentinian players had, particularly physically. There was this notion that we were small, not as fast. César insisted that this was not so, and drilled this into our heads. His main achievement, I think, was this effort he put in towards convincing us, truly making us believe, that we could travel anywhere and face opponents on their home grounds as equals.

On that tour we beat Poland – the Poland that had shone in the 1974 World Cup, beating Brazil to come third in the tournament with a very good-quality squad – on their home ground. And we beat the Soviets with a Mario Kempes goal that in some senses marked the dawn of the new Argentina. Certainly I think for us it constituted an extraordinary psychological push.

2

Footballer, Soldier, Student

I had come to Buenos Aires from the province of Córdoba (the second city in the country), where I was born and grew up. I am one of four brothers. Our father was a lawyer and we had a fairly normal middle-class childhood. In this sense I am quite different to most Argentinian football players who for the most part come from tougher socio-economic backgrounds.

Like most Argentinian boys I played football from a very young age, mostly in the street outside my house, and mostly with my older brothers. We lived in a safe neighbourhood, and the streets were wide. We played all the time. We would stop if a car drove by, then carry on. A neighbour who was quite fanatical about football, and who went on to enjoy watching me play at the highest level, gave us a couple of sets of goalposts. Soon the kids my age weren't enough of a challenge for me so

I played more and more with my eldest brothers, Tucho and Manuel, and their friends, who were almost seven years older than me. From seven to fourteen is a big age difference but I was already competent enough to handle them. It was an invaluable football education for me.

In Argentina it's very common for children to play what's known as *baby fútbol*, an official competition fairly well organized on a national basis, and I soon joined our local club, Junior. This wasn't just a football club but a 'club' club, a social institution where the members practised all sorts of sports and activities including tennis, basketball and hockey. My whole family were members, and my dad, as a lawyer, was also involved with the club's business, often acting as a consultant and giving them advice. I played most evenings and every weekend at Junior throughout my early childhood.

Another thing that is very common in Argentina is for football clubs to have kids' leagues – small sides of children who compete with other clubs before moving on to the lower divisions of the club itself. This is very well organized in Argentina. By the time I was about nine years old I had joined Instituto de Córdoba, one of the bigger clubs in the city (in football terms). Instituto had a particularly good kids' side at the time called

Estrella Roja (Red Star), and I played for them until I joined the youth divisions of Instituto at the age of thirteen. All the boys who played at the time went on to play First Division football. I remember most of them, but the one who stands out is Mario Kempes. Mario was a couple of years younger than me so we didn't play or train together early on, but we have known each other since back then.

I went to school in the morning – in Argentina, state schools are either morning shift or afternoon shift – then I ate and went out to play football. I always took it very seriously and knew I had potential. In fact, the truth is – and I don't find it easy to say this – I knew myself to be special from a very young age. I was technically gifted, and very comfortable with the ball at my feet. From as far back as I can remember I was winning best player and man of the match awards. I dreamt of playing for my country, and of winning the World Cup. The only doubt was whether my physique was cut out for it, because I was small.

I then got into Córdoba's best state secondary school, Montserrat, and that was a golden period of my life. My father had absolutely no interest in football, none – I think he probably saw me play for the first time when I was already turning out professionally for the first team – but he always took the attitude that as long as I studied and did well at school I could do anything I wanted. And I did study and do well at school, so I continued to spend all my free time playing football – every day, every afternoon after school, every evening and every weekend. As a teenager I never had a sense of what it was like to go out on a Saturday night. My friends started going out but I always had matches and had to concentrate and prepare. Football made me make certain choices in life. I also played table tennis, and won the provincial championship of Córdoba as a teenager. But football was my first choice from early on. In fact, it was an easy choice: there was no contest.

After I finished school I started studying law. Football was still very much there, of course, but it went hand in hand with a quest for a 'proper job', a career. Also, at the age of twenty, I was conscripted for military service. I was already fairly well known as a regular Instituto player so I managed to enjoy certain privileges and was able to do my military service stint as a cadet in the air force. My main task was to march soldiers to and from the infirmary, though I did have to do a night watch once which I remember as a particularly scary experience.

So in the mornings, from six to twelve, I was a soldier, marching, carrying arms, and obeying orders at HQ. Then I would have lunch at home and train with the Instituto first team in the afternoon. In the evenings I'd go to the law faculty at the university, where most of the other students were radically political, left wing, and organizing all sorts of activities. I think if it hadn't been for football I might have become politically active in some way; I was certainly curious and interested. But I had very little time for anything else.

These three worlds had absolutely nothing in common, but each one was completely soaked in the historical context of that time. In the Argentina of the early 1970s there was a very particular political climate: Juan Domingo Perón, who with his wife Eva (Evita) at his side had been an immensely popular president, was living in exile in Spain but a triumphal return was widely expected following intense activism by many of his supporters. Football would not escape being affected by this.

While I was doing my law degree I met a fellow student, Silvia Navarro, and we decided to prepare for an exam together: international law. But much more important than the subject and the studying or the passing (or not) of the exam (I did; she didn't) is the fact that I had met the love of my life and the woman who would be my friend and partner for the rest of my life. So I wasn't just footballer, soldier, student, but I was also embarking on the courtship for what would be a serious and long-lasting relationship.

Silvia and I were married in December 1973. Her father was a colonel in the army and made the chief of police in Córdoba at the time – an era of intense confrontation between left-wing guerillas and the government. As chief of police, he was not just a prime target but in the midst of a conflict which was both fraught and armed. Hence the amount of security surrounding our wedding, which was attended by all sorts of dignitaries including the archbishop of Córdoba and the governor of the province. I was already famous through football, but these people were not there for me.

Just two months after our wedding those same guests, those official dignitaries, were incarcerated by my father-in-law – the Buenos Aires government intervened in the province of Córdoba with all the institutional and constitutional implications this represented. I don't wish to dwell on the details of what became known as the *navarrazo* or the political complexities, rather to explain how our daily life took place in the thick of the tensions of the time. Once, while we were living at my father-in-law's house, we came under open fire – an attack sustained for ten minutes. On another occasion, while travelling with him in a motorcade, we again came under fire, this time by mistake from his own people. And all along I coexisted daily with the very different atmosphere of the law faculty.

It has to be said that although these people, these worlds, were fairly uninterested in my football life, it is one of the most amazing things about the sport, I think, that it opens doors and turns situations around all the time. I am always amazed by the power of football to do that. I was treated with a light hand both in the air force and at college in so many ways – higher grades, easier shifts, special dispensations. The sport also has power in terms of personal confidence. I have always been very shy, still am in many ways, not comfortable in groups or social situations. But football gave me an enormous boost and I found I could relax in so many different situations. The respect football earns you . . . in a sense I was seen as special, almost beyond criticism at times.

I don't know how it happened that the football part of this three-way lifestyle took over, but it did. It so happened that on the day I was discharged from military service – when medals are awarded and cadets are thanked for services rendered to the nation – I won a very prestigious award, best player of the interior, given out by *El Gráfico* magazine, Latin America's most established sports publication. I was nowhere to be found at the military ceremony because I was at *El Gráfico*'s awards party!

I stuck with law studies for a while longer. When I moved to Buenos Aires to play for Huracán, I moved with my law books under my arm and enrolled at the Buenos Aires law faculty. I did take another exam to get credits for one more subject, but I think I went at most three times to lectures. Once I joined the national squad I never found the time to study again. I never did finish my degree.

3

A Question Mark on My Back

I played in practically any and every position. I was a midfielder, of course, but in fact I could play in any and every position and my future turned out to prove that. I even played defensive sweeper when I went to QPR after Tottenham. At Instituto I was a midfielder but not defensive – there was always a player who was more defensive than me – but neither was I attacking, because I wasn't the number ten – the Maradona, the linkman, the creative midfielder. But according to what the team needed I would play more defensive or more offensive. What I did was whatever the team needed – always around the midfield of course, but if it was necessary to help the right-back I would go and help the right-back; if the left-back needed support I could go to him. Diego Maradona mentions me in his book as 'everyone's friend', and I think that's nicely put: I was always looking out for wherever our weakest point in defence was so that I could go and assist. And when attacking it was the same: when I saw we could do more on the right or the left, that we could put more pressure on when, say, Maradona or Mario Kempes was playing with me, I would run into those areas. It was something I decided myself. In principle I had to play on the right, and I remember some managers, especially the first few, being quite adamant about my sticking to the right. But I always played all over the pitch.

At Huracán I went on to the pitch wearing the number nine shirt (in the days when players wore shirts numbered one to eleven) but I wasn't a striker – far from it. I remember the manager there used to joke, 'You know what number you should be wearing on your strip? You should be wearing a question mark on your back!' No one knew what position I was. Even when I got to Tottenham. I remember one match early on, a Cup match, when an assistant to Keith Burkinshaw wanted more order in the ranks. This guy was big on formation. We were winning 2–0, I was playing very well and so was the team, and he was angry at half-time because we hadn't stuck to the formation. 'What about the formation?' I said. 'We're 2–0 up, playing amazingly . . . Why change?'

This was all learning I'd incorporated into my play way back at Instituto. Back then, if the number ten was injured I would go on for the number ten; if the number five was injured I could take on the role of the number five. At Instituto my number was eight, but I wasn't a normal number eight because the traditional Argentinian number eight stuck more to the flanks, going up and down on the right without being totally offensive or totally defensive, whereas I would run around all over the pitch. I learned at a very young age that a lot could be achieved on a pitch by moving around intelligently. The aim then was to try and reach the front – to be not the creator but somehow the builder of the team. I played very different to that. It feels arrogant to say it now, but with hindsight I can see I was somehow ahead of my time.

In those days Argentinian football teams were incredibly stereotyped. Basically, they all played the same, mostly 4-4-2. But I was never stereotyped. I was never on the bench, but I did sometimes cause problems for my managers, especially the ones who wanted to play me in a particular place and used to say 'stay there'. Of course, every now and then we would have a bad result and I took the flak. But on the whole my system worked.

My first match with Instituto, I remember, was

against Talleres – the big Córdoba derby. The right-wing was injured so I went on as a right-wing. Me! That's not my game at all, staying on the wings and crossing balls – not me. So immediately, even in that first match, I was running all over the pitch, down the left, down the right, getting into every nook and cranny I could find.

To some extent I was inspired – or perhaps it was more like corroboration from outside for my beliefs – by Holland in 1974. I remember watching them in the World Cup and thinking, 'These guys are great!' There were exceptional players in the side, like Cruyff, but actually it wasn't so much what the individuals were doing as what they were achieving as a team – you know, the 'total' concept, the way they all moved all over the pitch.

I think in football terms three people have been very important in my life – huge influences. The first was a man called Santiago Semino who was our trainer in the little league but kept moving up with us, year after year. So I had him when I was thirteen, fourteen, fifteen and so on. He knew a lot about football – eventually he became president of Instituto, actually. Semino understood my way of playing and he never imposed any sort of limit on my game.

The second was César Menotti, who turned me into

a full-blown international. I was already a good player by the time I made the national squad – I was top player the year I joined Huracán, for example, and the winner of awards and so on – and playing with established players, but Menotti elevated my status to truly international quality.

And the third was Keith Burkinshaw at Spurs.

And in all honesty I can say that not one of them ever instructed me about what I had to do on a pitch. They made comments, of course, gave indications, but what it essentially came down to was trust: every match has a life of its own, and these three men trusted me to make the best possible decision on the pitch at any given time, based on what the team needed, what the circumstances required. Even later in my career, when playing with Diego Maradona, for example, I was still doing this. In many senses playing with Diego was easy: all you needed to do was get the ball to him, because Diego was truly spectacular. But sometimes he was incredibly tightly marked, and when that happened I took on the responsibility of creating. And that was basically just a natural progression from what I had learned as a very young boy at Instituto. And I had understood it very clearly back then.

We were all good, even at the age of thirteen, but I made it first (not counting Kempes, who came from another town). I think there were a couple of things that allowed me to stand out from the others. One was the obsession with the number ten. Everyone wanted to be a number ten. All the best players in every team wore the number ten: Pelé, my idol at River Plate, Ermindo Onega, Independiente's Ricardo Bochini, 'El Beto' Alonso (also at River Plate), José Daniel Valencia (Talleres de Córdoba), Ricardo Villa . . . they were all number tens. But in those days a number ten didn't wear overalls, he wore a smoking jacket, if you see what I mean. They would hang about in the shade and if the ball wasn't passed to them they wouldn't roll their sleeves up and work for it. I wasn't like that. I sought the ball.

The other thing was my mental grasp of football. I was good technically, but when I compared myself to some team-mates there were quite a few who were superior to me. I was, however, always able to learn from them. If I saw someone perfecting a particular technique, whatever it might have been, I would practise that same technique until I got it under control.

But what really marked the difference between me and the others was the way in which I saw football. As I got better and played more and more I also got marked more and more. I used to be singled out, man to man at times. So it was absolutely crucial for me to start wandering wherever I could sneak in, probing for the weakness in my opponent.

Like a snake. My brother Manuel thought I moved around the pitch like one and gave me the nickname *Pitón* (Python). It stuck, even though I thought it completely wrong, because a python is a large snake. If anything I was more like the *culebra*, a much smaller snake.

4

The Changing Face of Argentina

As a boy, I had a dream of being the best. As time passed, that dream, in which I saw myself playing for Argentina, saw myself winning the World Cup, got closer and closer to becoming a reality.

By 1974 I was already an experienced player. Although I had only played in Córdoba, I had some experience of top club clashes, having featured in matches against River and Boca. I was about to be transferred to Huracán, one of the best clubs in the country at the time. And I'd just seen Holland play in the World Cup and been blown away by the Clockwork Orange team effort.

Argentina, however, had returned from the World Cup humiliated. As I said before, we always thought we were so good, the best. The 1974 World Cup was a wake-up call. Menotti was appointed national manager that December. He'd been in charge at Huracán when they won the Argentinian championship in 1973 and had managed some outstanding players at club level: Houseman, Miguel Angel Brindisi, Carlos Babington and Carrascosa, for instance, who all played for Argentina. In fact the president of Huracán, David Bracuto, was also the president of the Argentinian Football Association (AFA), and he gave the national job to Menotti.

When César started work in 1975 he created two *selecciones*, two squads basically: a youth one, which included players like Alberto Tarantini, Passarella, and Américo Gallego; and another which was known as the 'interior squad', which consisted mainly of players from the provinces like Daniel Valencia, Luis Galván and Miguel Oviedo. I was in that second squad, and at the end of the year I won the top player award.

Initially, my inclusion in the squad was not in doubt (so long as my good form continued, that was). Menotti had a soft spot for me; in fact they used to call me 'son of Menotti' as a way of teasing me now and again. There weren't many surprises in that initial squad, even Mario Kempes, who was already playing for Valencia in Spain. César had said he would only pick players who were in Argentina, but Mario was the exception to this rule.

But I think César's work with the new Argentina

started in earnest in 1976 with a tour of Europe, which was a real turning point. Under César, a whole load of the nonsense that had gone on before stopped. Throwing oneself on the ground to waste time was a no-no. Are you injured? No? Then get up and carry on playing. He was also against fouling. He departed so much from what our domestic football had become. And we started to get known around the world. We earned ourselves a reputation; everyone wanted to play against us. Our sense of self-respect grew hand in hand with this international reputation, and we got over that sense that we were inferior. We faced all opponents as equals.

At that time the Soviet Union was *the* Soviet Union. We were struck, mostly, by how incredibly strange the food was, and by the fact that there was no Coca-Cola at the hotel. In Ukraine, for example, where we were meant to be staying at the best hotel, we were shocked by the fact that we had to make our own beds. These were all little things which we observed from an anecdotal point of view rather than to make some sort of profound reflection on the state of the world. Profe Pizarotti, who did everything from sorting out the kits to all the physical training, and who was a very important figure in the build-up to and during the 1978 World Cup, organized an outing to Red Square one day.

As it was on a free day, those who wanted to come along could, but it was a choice. It's always that way. As a football player you get used to travelling to all sorts of places and all you get to see is the airport, the stadium and that's about it. Rarely do players go and visit some place of interest, though I usually did if I could. For most of the squad it was football, football, football. Very little else got a look-in.

During that tour of Eastern Europe, on 24 March 1976 to be precise, when we were due to play against Hungary in Budapest, a military coup took place in Argentina. There are a few well-known facts and we can state them as they are. Juan Perón had died in 1974, a year after returning to the country. His third wife Isabel became President, but the country soon descended into economic and political chaos. Everyone, it seemed, was clamouring for a coup, and the military government, under General Videla, was accepted with open arms. I don't remember exactly what we heard or how we heard about it while we were abroad, but the fact is that when we returned home Argentina was under military rule.

Everything was normal; people just carried on with their lives. If you were a journalist you continued doing your journalism; the lawyer continued practising law; and the footballer just played football. Nothing had changed in Argentina on the surface. The only thing that had changed was the guy who ruled the roost. He was now imposed on us rather than elected, but in those days that's what happened in Latin America all the time: democratic governments alternated with military governments. Argentina wasn't necessarily different at this time for having had a coup.

It was only later, in the early eighties, when the military government fell and talk started about 'the disappeared', that people started to ask us footballers, 'Did you know?' as if we were somehow complicit. We knew something, as some of us read the newspapers of the time – *El Clarín*, *La Nación*, *La Crónica*. We watched TV, too. But where were all the great institutions of the time? Where was the archbishop, the Catholic Church, the judges, the press? What were they saying? Nobody said anything. So us, footballers, football players, how were we to know more? What we knew, thought about and worried about was the next match.

There were characters who were later said to be more politicized. Jorge Carrascosa, for example, who played at Huracán with me. The captain, a guy with a great personality, half philosopher, he was a very close friend of mine. Nobody knows for certain why he decided not to play in the 1978 World Cup. It was said that there were political reasons, but never by him. It was also said that it was because Kempes came to join the squad, because César had said no players would come from abroad. There were a lot of Argentinian players abroad – Osvaldo Piazza in France, Brindisi in Spain, Babington in Germany – but César had said it was going to be a team with only Argentina-based players. Carrascosa resigned from the national squad when he was the captain.

César had some left-wing ideas, Guevarist almost, but I don't think he ever took part in a demonstration. And we really didn't talk about these things because César . . . well, who would he talk about it with? Actually, the only one at the time would have been me. I did have some sort of political curiosity, and concern. I read the newspapers, and not just the sports pages. Leopoldo Luque, Mario, Gallego . . . if you tried to discuss politics with them they would snap, 'What are you coming to bust my balls for?' And remember, at the time nobody talked about 'the disappeared'. Nobody knew. I can clearly remember arriving in England, going to a Catholic church and picking up a leaflet by Amnesty International, denouncing Argentina for state terrorism. It sounded awful.

As I said, there were many institutions that should have been speaking out but all they said through the late seventies and into the eighties was 'nothing's going on, everything's fine'. I didn't say anything either. After all, everything was back to normal in Argentina after the coup, as I've already explained. Yet somehow people never stopped asking why we didn't denounce the military takeover.

But we were just football players.

5

Doubts and Pressure

I think Menotti must have been under an incredible amount of pressure, but he didn't let it seep through to us. We were completely focused on football. After the tour to Europe we all went back to our clubs but carried on spending a lot of time together, training mostly, and playing friendly matches. Preparing for the World Cup was the number one priority. As host nation we were already qualified but we needed to make sure we were up to the challenge. History was against us, on the World Cup stage.

I had arrived in Buenos Aires to play for Huracán already married to Silvia and with our first child Pablo already born, carrying my law books under my arm. But football trumped law school early on. The year 1976 was all about football. At club level we were on a roll. Huracán did extremely well in the league. We beat

San Lorenzo (our main derby) 5–0 at home and 5–1 away. We had more points than any other club. We weren't champions that season because of the way this particular tournament was organized: in the final we found ourselves against Boca, where they beat us 1–0 in a very wet and muddy Estadio Monumental, but overall we had twelve points more than Boca. Then, in 1977, with five players gone from the club on international duty, Huracán were fighting relegation. The priority of the national team was so much emphasized that, for example, in 1978 I didn't play a single game for Huracán. But the five of us who had joined the international squad were thriving. There was enormous interest from the press all over the world. And the internal dynamics of things related to the squad, money and everything, took over. There were a lot of egos around, and a lot of quite difficult characters.

César was very lyrical; he loved to talk and philosophize. The day-to-day activities were mostly the Profe's task. He managed everything related to discipline, too, and lived the same life we did. He used to allow us one glass of wine at meal times, the idea being that wine was better than Coca-Cola. And he would put one bottle of wine every four places at the table. I never drank, actually. When I came to live in England I think the most I'd ever had in my whole life were a couple of whiskys. He died fairly recently, Profe Pizarotti. The truth is, the work he did with us was spectacularly good. I never heard him make a single comment about football, though. He just didn't get involved. That was César's area – and César would not permit anybody to talk about football with us.

But there were other aspects about football in Argentina that were very badly handled. For instance, River and Boca were refusing to release their players for the national team – César wanted us a lot of the time – and it was so badly handled at a national level, or rather a federative level, that in River's case it ended up being the players themselves who chose. Norberto Alonso, for instance, chose his club, River, whereas Daniel Passarella opted for the national squad. J. J. López, who was the best player in Argentina that year and an extraordinary footballing talent, stayed with River. (J. J. should have been included in the squad, of course, but from my point of view in many ways he threatened to be my nemesis, being direct competition for my place. I think, though, that both of us should have been in the squad as we were the best midfielders in Argentina.) The fight with River over the players got nastier and César soon got tired of dealing with it.

The choice was entirely football driven, I think, for the players. Our salaries were paid by the Argentinian

Football Association (AFA). César had managed to agree they could cover this for as long as he wanted us. But as a squad we had become incredibly prestigious. We played a match against River at the Estádio Monumental, which in those days was just the River stadium; national matches were still played at Boca's Bombonera. We filled the stadium. If the national squad had before then been grossing, say, $10,000 per match, we went on to take in $100,000, $500,000. There was an exponential increase in the premium for our squad. Sponsors, advertising deals, it all started rolling in. The national side became an incredibly lucrative deal for the AFA.

At the time I had absolutely no idea about any of this. Zero. There had always been problems around prize money, that was typical. There were always some individuals trying to do better than others, always someone going, 'I'm not playing for that money.' And there were meetings to discuss these issues. Daniel Passarella, Leopoldo Luque and me were the ones who usually fought our corner with the Argentinian Football Association, though Daniel didn't speak out much over the bonuses. But César had even managed to change all that for the better. Before Menotti, no one had ever discussed how much money the players would get for winning the final or even the semi-final. What was always argued and negotiated, what everyone concentrated on, was how much money there would be for getting through the first stage, and then how much for getting past the second round; beyond that no one looked. Under César, for the first time it was agreed that if we were knocked out in the first phase we wouldn't get a penny. Everything was geared towards complete success. It was another of Menotti's great changes: he set our sights on the final.

There were all sorts of other problems. For example, an advertising campaign might request specific players: this one, this one and this one. Then what should we do? Divide the money among the whole squad? And invariably someone would emerge asking for more money, some star would come with more demands. At one point problems like these got serious.

Adidas had particular contracts with some players, and the national squad was adidas, but a lot of the players – even César – had deals with Puma. I'd had a deal with adidas since my Huracán days, but as we became more and more coveted the deals and the conflicts got bigger. If we played, the whole country watched – and sometimes matches were even televised in Europe. Basically, it was a squad whose members were all earning different amounts and getting different rewards – logically, that leads to problems.

After the excitement and success of 1976, 1977 was a

complicated year. We played a lot of international matches, we had a series of bad results, and doubts started to be aired. People started questioning Menotti's confidence, whether or not we would make it. Many members of the squad came under harsh criticism. When Carrascosa resigned the critics intensified their attacks. There was clamour – actually, at the time it seemed to me like an enormous wave of public opinion – for J. J. López to play in my place; people saw it as stubborn of César to stick with me. So I came under particular fire, but the critics aimed their words at the squad as a whole.

I wasn't playing well, I know that, but I wasn't used to my status as a member of the team being questioned. Everywhere I went I was told I shouldn't be in the squad – everywhere: even in Córdoba! Then *Goles* magazine published a cover which was a picture of me with a huge cross over it. And that made me feel so bad. It was the worst time of my life so far: it was make or break for me. I was truly doubtful that I would be able to cope, and I was on the brink of tendering my resignation.

During this period I remember watching West Germany – they too were having a bad run of results and had started losing some matches. I saw Franz Beckenbauer, one of my idols, make a couple of mistakes and the people started booing him. Every time he touched the ball, boos from the crowd. And of course as I watched him I saw he was getting worse, making more mistakes. I thought, 'If he can't play under that pressure, how am I going to?'

Over time a version of the 1978 World Cup story has established itself, and it says that nobody put any pressure on Menotti or the team. But the pressure we were under in 1977 and 1978 was monstrous. It was a test for all of us, a baptism of fire. We were not playing that well as a team and the people weren't convinced. In those months leading up to the competition nine international teams came to play against us at the Boca stadium – in part as a sort of recce for the World Cup, but also because we ranked highly as an adversary and everyone wanted to play against us. Of all those squads the strongest by far was West Germany, the reigning world champions. And also England, mostly because of everything they represented in football terms. They had some great players, like Kevin Keegan, Trevor Brooking and Ray Clemence.

Boca were doing incredibly well at the time but there were hardly any Boca players in the national squad. Sections of the press started to run with a campaign suggesting that Boca manager Toto Lorenzo should be in charge of Argentina. So when we played at the Boca stadium the home crowd would boo us. I found that very difficult. Even when they read our names out, before we came out of the tunnel, we could hear the crowd whistling and booing. We lost against West Germany, 3–1; they won the game fair and square. We managed to draw against England and Scotland, 1–1 in both games, but it wasn't good enough and we came under more scrutiny and criticism.

I talked about it with Ricky Villa, Mario and Daniel, telling them I was thinking of quitting. They said, '*Tranquilo*' – stay calm. It was definitely one of the most testing times of my life, without a doubt: either I soldiered on and played the World Cup or I left and just continued being one of so many good players in the Argentinian league. Then César put me on the bench, against Brazil no less, at the Maracanã. Me, on the bench? I was never on the bench. In fact, that would prove to be the only time in my entire international career.

We lost 2–0 against Brazil so I was back in the side. But I still wasn't playing good football. The manager at Huracán even spoke to me about it, confirming that César was having doubts about me. Me, the so-called son of Menotti? But I could feel I wasn't cutting it. And the more I felt the lack of trust and faith of my own people the worse I played. I think maybe some players find adversity a motivator, but the way I felt at that time was far from motivating.

And then we went to Peru, whose national side at the time was an important team. This was regarded as a difficult match. They were at home, yet we turned the bad tide, winning 3–1 and making them sweat. And more importantly, I played very well.

Obviously everyone had watched the match and suddenly people were talking highly of me again. By the time Peru came to play against us in the return leg at the Bombonera, a few days later, I was feeling a lot more confident. This was early 1978, and it was on that pitch that I took the calculated risk against Teófilo Cubillas which perhaps defined the rest of my career – my life even. One nutmeg can change a whole life!

6

Diego

In a sense I think I had something to do with the fact that Diego Maradona didn't play in the 1978 World Cup. I'm not directly responsible, of course, and I wasn't personally involved in any way. But looking back now it's possible to see not only the turning points in my life but the long-term impact of single events that at the time maybe did not feel so significant. The significance of a moment is something we are only able to assess a long time after the event.

In the run-up to the World Cup Menotti had put together a working squad of twenty-five players. We were all released from our clubs and stayed in José C. Paz, a city just outside Buenos Aires where our training headquarters, in a private villa, were. There was a starting squad, which more or less picked itself, and then the substitutes, who called themselves *la selección fantasma*

– the ghost squad. They were very good-natured about it, and as it turned out, throughout the World Cup campaign if one of them played they would all celebrate. There was a nice dynamic between us and the ghost squad. In reality we were all one squad, and a very well-formed group at that, very tight. But the time soon came for César to make his final squad selection, for which he had to choose twenty-two from the twenty-five.

During the build-up we'd also played against youth sides, and Diego Maradona had been among them from the outset. He was already almost impossible to mark. (I and Américo Gallego, who was very astute, an exceptional player, took great care to learn more about his way of playing so that we could mark him effectively in training. So when Diego played against Gallego or me we managed to guess his moves more often than most people could.) By early 1978 Diego was one of the twenty-five and had been playing with us for a while. His debut with the first team came in February 1977 against Hungary – he came on for Ricky, I think – and when that run of international matches in which we'd had such a hard time had finished, Diego was one of the squad. He got better every match. He was just sixteen, going on seventeen, and even though to start off with he maybe wasn't up to the same level as some of us, he improved all the time. In fact, exactly one year after the World Cup we played against Holland in Berne and Diego was already by far the best player out of the twenty-two men on the pitch, perhaps already the number one in the world.

Diego is very intelligent. He always wanted to learn, asked questions, had an eagerness to improve all the time. He saw a move and five minutes later was perfecting it to the point of being better than whoever he was emulating. He saw something he liked, a beautifully executed dummy, for example, and then he did it too. When training finished Diego stayed behind, shooting endlessly at the goal – *pum, pum, pum*. And, naturally, he kept getting better and better at it.

With the benefit of hindsight, it's clear that he did go on to become the best player ever, in my opinion, so it makes sense to analyse why he was such a great footballer. I think he has one of the biggest hearts I've come across in my life. I mean, as a team player. He was always 100 per cent available to the team, and focused when on the pitch. He could have however many thousands of problems off the pitch (indeed most of the time he did) but he could forget them all when it came to playing. He fought with the AFA president; with FIFA he disputed money terms with various people; he had women troubles; he had particularly big fights with the press – everything you can imagine. Yet whatever was going on around him, when the whistle blew, that was it. On the pitch, he existed only for his team-mates.

I would never have been able to perform under such circumstances. I've always found it a fundamental, crucial necessity to have a harmonious life. When, years later, I was in France, for instance, I played badly – I had never imagined I would be capable of playing so badly – because of all the problems I was having off the pitch. Which is how I know I would never have been able to cope with the sort of pressure Diego was under. But he was unusually capable of existing only for his team-mates, and in the early months of 1978 he was one of us. Focusing on his football, improving with every training session, every match, totally determined to remain in the final squad.

But César had three surplus players, and there were five players for whom it was a case of maybe yes, maybe no. It was obvious that being left out would be one of the biggest disappointments of Diego's life. He was going to become the best player in the world, and even then there was absolutely no reason to think he wouldn't. Neither is there any reason to think we wouldn't have won the World Cup with Diego in the squad. But back then he was very young, and some of us were more established, undisputed choices for the first team. Mario, Luque, Passarella and me, for instance – it was obvious we were going to start. Looking back it was probably a mistake of Menotti not to include him in the squad.

Daniel Passarella was the captain. He was very much our leader on the pitch. I think off it some of us maybe spoke more, were more vociferous, and Menotti had others who were his 'lieutenants', if I can put it like that. But on the pitch Daniel had exceptional motivation, a very personal drive, a strong character and personality. When he stepped on the pitch he underwent a trans-formation. He was a born winner; winning was the only thing that interested him. And he transmitted that to the rest of us when playing in our team; as an opponent, however, he was something to contend with! I played against him at club level: I was with Huracán, he was at River, and he practically broke me in two. But when he was on our side he brought fighting spirit to the team. In that sense he was hugely important throughout the tournament. And he was an extraordinary player. He played three World Cups in fact, 1978, 1982 and 1986. Well, in Mexico in 1986 he got sick, but he would have been very important in that competition as well. His inbuilt winning streak was crucial but he also had a physical potency that was impressive. Even though he wasn't tall he could jump and he was excellent in the air. He scored loads of headers. He was a superb defender, too, always positioning himself in the right place. He's certainly one of the best defenders I've ever played with.

Mario Kempes was also established as a super player, having already featured in a World Cup, in 1974. Menotti might have said he would build the squad solely with Argentina-based players, but he made an exception with Mario because he was deemed indispensable.

Three decades after the disappointment of being excluded from the 1978 World Cup squad, Diego was appointed the manager of Argentina. I am asked all the time for my opinions, which somehow have the benefit of 'insider knowledge'. I would like to say first of all that I believe in him. It's a risky appointment, sure, but I think he can provide the necessary inspiration for the young players. If someone tells you to do something it's not the same as if Diego Maradona tells you to do that particular thing. However, with Diego it is always all or nothing, and in that sense it's a risky appointment. In March 2009, Juan Román Riquelme decided to quit the national team became of a dispute with Diego. The headlines and the editorials provided endless suggestions but it was all speculation. In all probability a number of minor issues accumulated, unplanned near misses and minor spats which seem of no importance in themselves, then the cumulative effect became one big drama. It's not the same thing as with Carrascosa. We don't know now whether in thirty years' time Riquelme's story will be as much of a big deal.

But with Diego, his exclusion from the 1978 World Cup acquired legendary significance, just as his whole life did. We didn't know then just how good he was going to be, just how big things were going to get for him in football. Back then he was an extraordinarily talented kid who was easily as good as the best of the slightly older, more experienced professionals.

And that's why I say, looking back on events thirty-plus years on, that maybe I was partly the reason why Diego missed out on the 1978 World Cup. Because during those days when César was making his mind up, in a training match against the ghost squad, I tackled Ricky Villa studs up.

Ricky was a superbly skilled attacking midfielder. We had played together a lot in the interior squad and had become close friends already. But he wasn't in the first team so we played against each other in this particular training session, and I went for the ball but accidentally got his leg. César didn't really approve of tackles, least of all in training, so this was really bad; if one of the other team had come on to one of us, the starting eleven, the way I did on Ricky, there would have been hell to pay. But I *was* going for the ball; it was just that I was trying out some special new boots adidas had recently brought from France and I slipped and got Ricky on the shin. I practically cut his leg open and he was out for a while. As a matter of fact it was touch and go whether he would be ready for the World Cup itself.

If my studs had gone a fraction of an inch further into Ricky's flesh, he might not have recovered in time to play. And if Ricky had been left out of the tournament, Diego's name would have been on that final list.

But it didn't turn out that way.

7

Analyse Like a Computer

A few years ago I spent a day with Leopoldo Luque. I noticed Leo remembered everything from the 1978 World Cup in enormous detail. He still lives the experience vividly. I'm not like that. I feel things and move on. Time moves on, and life must continue. I never stay in a moment, no matter how amazing or special it was. Maybe I'm cold, or maybe there is an 'old man' syndrome that just hasn't hit me yet, but I really don't want to endlessly relive a moment that has gone. My mind analyses more like a computer: it scans the facts and hopes to learn from an experience with a view to the future.

There are details about the World Cup, even the final, that I don't remember. The end of the match, the events that followed the final whistle, for example: I don't remember anything about this, absolutely nothing.

Who hugged me? Who did I celebrate with? How did I celebrate? I know I lifted the trophy. Obviously. I know, too, that we did a victory lap, but only because I've seen it on TV since. But I don't have that emotional sensation of living the moment again through my memories. And when I say I've seen footage of the final on TV, well, obviously over the past few decades certain images have become inevitable. But it's not like I generally watch a match over and over again once it's been played. I've never done that, not even with Spurs games.

Having said that, I feel extremely proud of having been part of that squad, very proud of my team-mates. As a group we were united, exceptionally close, and as a consequence we overcame so many things that happened during the tournament itself. A case in point is Luque's experience: his brother died after one match, and not only that but Leo also suffered a serious injury. And we were able to support one another, to support him. He carried on playing. It must have been agony for him. I see it as an absolute example of what that group was like.

I feel grateful for the support we received from one another, from the people, from the technical team. I think it played a huge part in our being able to achieve our dream, because our challenge was spectacularly huge: it wasn't just to participate in the tournament but to come out of it as champions. Our aim was to win the World Cup on home soil.

It's a shame that since then the tournament has become such a tainted event – the political backdrop and other allegations of foul play have taken a lot away from the amazing football experience it was. Obviously at the time we had no idea how controversial it all was in the rest of the world. We Argentinians were 'Human and Right' – that was the slogan on some stickers issued by the government when a human rights commission came to visit the country – and that was all we knew.

There was no free press, so the press went along with government propaganda, and I admit I believed it 100 per cent – I sincerely thought there was some sort of conspiracy against Argentina. Maybe one has to be a bit Argentinian to understand this, but we always felt at some subliminal level that we were somehow chosen by God, that we were such a great country, so full of natural riches, that the rest of the world were jealous of us. Of course one need only step out of the country for a minute to realize this is not so, but that's a little bit how the Argentinian psyche works. And I believed it all at the time.

Argentina had been named host country of the

World Cup long before the military government took over. Obviously, once they were in power they decided to use the competition to their political advantage. What's also obvious, in my opinion, is that any government would do the same, no matter what kind of regime or political persuasion. In a country like Argentina, where football means so much to so many people, the government was always going to manipulate the event in order to gain popularity.

Our day-to-day life throughout the tournament was far removed from political thoughts, however. We were oblivious to how controversial the World Cup might be elsewhere and had no sense that there might be pressures from outside on Menotti or the squad. As far as we were concerned, it was all about the football.

It was as if we had been encapsulated. We lived in a *concentrated* way. We were always in the training camp or hotel, spent all our time together, totally separate from our families, and our minds were occupied with a single mission: we wanted to win the World Cup. I didn't personally feel any pressure from outside the camp, and I doubt any of my team-mates did. Did Menotti? I imagine so, but he never let us take it on board. He was the one who contained us in this 'capsule', because he knew it was absolutely crucial that we focus entirely on the football.

For the month of the tournament it was like we were in a vortex, the hustle and bustle of all things football increasing as things got underway. The press, the TV, all anyone talked about was football. Of course there was pressure on us in strictly football terms, which is why I think Menotti got it so right by keeping us isolated and focused. If we had been out in the streets among the people things would have got very difficult. We felt affection and warmth from the people, we felt that very strongly, but the main thing was that we still had our time to ourselves, our own space to train and get on with our thing.

Our remit was to win the World Cup, but our actual objective – what we were confident we could achieve, and the least we expected from ourselves – was to get to the final. By the time the World Cup kicked off we had done most of the work and felt that all that remained was to play the matches. We were convinced we had every chance of making it to the final. If we then won it – well, even better. But anything short of playing the final would have been a failure.

We were based outside Buenos Aires to start with, in José C. Paz. Another World Cup venue was Rosario Central's stadium, which had the advantage of being smaller than the Monumental (River Plate's stadium). The Monumental had been refurbished completely for the World Cup and at the time was state of the art, but it had a running track around the pitch and although the capacity was larger than Rosario's, the crowd was further away. In Rosario, although capacity was probably forty thousand down, the fans were practically on top of the players, and of course if you're the home team the advantage is huge because that's intimidating for the visiting team.

So when we lost 1–0 against Italy in Buenos Aires in the first round of group matches we weren't overly concerned, because the defeat meant we had to go to Rosario for the second-round group ties. Also, the loss didn't take us away from our main objective because we were already through to the second round.

Our first match in Rosario was against Poland. We played well and won 2–0. Ubaldo 'El Pato' Fillol saved a penalty, which was a huge boost to our confidence. But I'm not prone to thinking that this match was more important than that one, or that result was more significant than another. I think all the matches we played in that World Cup were important. Our subsequent game against Brazil was massive, as was the clash with France during the first round. In fact the biggest test for our nerves was probably the opening match, against Hungary. Most people would name the climax, the final against Holland, as the most significant, but I don't feel compelled to relive that game or any of the matches we played along the way. As I said, it just so happens that some people remain fixated on the big events of their lives, the main matches in their careers. For me, life is more of a continuum, football just a part of life.

The experience of playing in the 1978 World Cup was invaluable. The human side of the squad, the way we gelled, and Menotti's football teachings have marked me both personally and professionally. The friends I made . . . I shared a room with Ricky Villa; and then Mario Kempes, who joined the squad a little later, from Europe, occupied a small annexe to our room because he didn't have someone to be paired with. First thing in the morning Mario would reach out from the bed for his cigarettes and ashtray! Mario ended up being Player of the Year in 1978. He was a big man, pure potency, with an exquisite touch. In fact, very few of his goals were scored with pure power alone. In my opinion Mario is the best Argentinian player of all time – apart from Diego. This is how highly I rate him. It is a pity that this status, recognized all over the world, is not recognized in Argentina because of the 'Diego phenomenon'. That entire month, living, eating and breathing football, was a joyous experience. I'm very proud to have been a part of it and I have nothing but respect for my team-mates and the technical staff. But I don't feel it's the be-all and end-all of my life. I don't feel defined by it, that that's my story. On the contrary, my life, I felt, was just beginning.

8

The Fix

I do, however, have to talk about the second-round match against Peru as it has aroused so much suspicion since. According to the group we were in, and because of the television schedule, some games were being played at different times. Our match against Peru, for instance, was played after Brazil's tie with Poland. Which meant we knew the result we needed. Since then FIFA has dictated that under such circumstances both matches should kick-off at the same time. Which is how it should be. But in those days it wasn't like that. I think a big factor was that we were in South America and the match schedules were ruled to a large extent by European TV audiences.

I think we even watched the first half of that Brazil–Poland game before taking the bus to the stadium for our match. We heard the result once we were there – 3–1 to the Brazilians. The way things worked, the two winners of the second-round groups would progress to the final and the two runners-up would go straight to the third-place play-off, so we knew as we prepared to meet Peru that to get to the final we needed to win by four clear goals. It was a pretty tall order but we were confident. Of course it wasn't going to be easy, but we had faith in ourselves.

I didn't play in that match, having picked up an ankle injury against Brazil; a lot of people's main memories of Ricky Villa during the 1978 World Cup come from that game. I remember Ricky doing an awful foul. He was booked but he should have been sent off – and not just sent off the pitch but sent out of the country! It's an indication of the nature of the game that Ricky fouled someone so badly, because it's not his style. Ricky doesn't know how to kick people. It was a small incident but it has stuck with me because it's a marker for just how heated the match was – quite typical of the time that the games were more like wars – and also because when Ricky and I arrived in London a lot of people recalled the foul. Which is kind of funny.

The match against Peru was also a bitterly fought encounter, quite dirty. There was no flow to it and I found it quite ugly, which is a shame because on the pitch were two potentially brilliant teams. There were rumours in Argentina at the time claiming the Brazilians had offered the Peruvian players houses, cars, all manner of riches if they beat us. That was the only rumour we heard. Until match day we had never heard any other rumour about anything else. Certainly when the game started it wasn't looking so good for us. I remember Peru's Juan Oblitas took a shot which went very close and famously hit the post – I say this to emphasize that our victory wasn't as easy as the eventual scoreline might suggest. Over time it has also been said that our victory was somehow arranged at a presidential level between the two countries. I am certain, absolutely certain, that no one in our squad, technical staff or players, had anything to do with fixing the match, or any knowledge of a fix. I can't, of course, speak for the military government under President Videla, which we later learned was capable of terrible things.

Always there is a latent question in football: is it possible to fix a match? I think it's possible to influence a referee. I've witnessed decisions that are so absurd they're inexplicable, but if you ask me if I've ever been involved in a match in which the official has been explicitly influenced, the answer is no. I have been involved in so many encounters, as a player and as a manager, that there could well have been a match fixed somewhere along the line. But I have absolutely no knowledge or even suspicion of any foul play in a particular match. I've never been aware of it at the time, or known after or before, or even heard about it.

No one has ever accused the referee of that Argentina–Peru game of any wrongdoing, but the finger, as I said, has been pointed at the government. Is that possible? Of course. Remember, that regime was capable of 'disappearing' thirty thousand people; why would they stop at a little football match? What's one more spot to the tiger, as we say in Argentina? But I don't think the junta did it. My personal opinion is that they didn't, not because they wouldn't, but because they couldn't. It would have had to be a fix between the presidents or the governments, and somehow it would have had to trickle down to the players, which is too difficult.

The other person who over the years has been subject to most accusations is Ramón Quiroga, the Peruvian goalkeeper. He was born in Argentina, and his style of goalkeeping was risky: a bit like Hugo Gatti, he would come far out of his area, leaving the goal exposed. The fact that he was born in Argentina was just one of those crossroads life throws at folk. He could have said 'I can't play against Argentina', for example, but he never did. Football, like life, often presents us with scenarios full of conflict. Quiroga may have been a native Argentinian but he took his professional life as a Peruvian in his stride. It would have made more sense for him to succeed as the Peruvian goalkeeper than to throw a match of that calibre out of some sense of loyalty to his country of birth.

I don't believe that match against Peru was fixed. It's an opinion – I have no knowledge of the facts. What I do know is what we saw and felt that day. We knew we needed to score at least four goals without reply and we didn't expect it to be easy but we were confident. More than confident: we were convinced we could beat Peru by the required margin. We had the past experience of those two matches a few months before the World Cup where we had been the better team, so at no point did we feel 'oh, that's not doable'. We were a little nervous, of course, knowing that ideally we needed to score in the first half at least twice, but we felt it was doable.

The match itself wasn't easy, but we did it. In spite of Oblitas's shot, which could have paved the way for a different outcome altogether, we ended up beating Peru 6–0. After the match Videla came into the dressing room with his guest, Henry Kissinger, who was very involved in United States soccer. That was the first time we saw our President: we had never been to the Casa

Rosada (Argentina's White House), he had never come to our training camp, there had been no contact. We had just got through to the World Cup Final so it was fairly unremarkable that the leader of the nation might come in to congratulate us and bring his VIP along. We were celebrating anyway, in the showers, some half naked, some completely naked, singing away. It was party time for us. We'd just achieved our objective and booked a place in the final.

I imagine Videla must have said something like 'well done, lads', something along those lines, but I honestly can't remember. Kissinger didn't say anything at all. At that moment we were euphoric, celebrating our results on the pitch so far and feeling we were steps away from glory. We knew nothing about rumours of a fix, about governments dealing behind our backs, and, as I said, I firmly believe there was nothing untoward in the match – and not because I think the military regime had any moral scruples about it. I have often said that if ever proof of a fix was produced I would give back my medal. Under such circumstances our World Cup victory would not mean anything to me.

9

The Final

The fact is we made it to the final. After the Peru match we went back to our training camp in Rosario, we all had dinner together, and the next day we returned to the *concentración*, the headquarters in José C. Paz, to start working. Did I say 'working'? I mean training for the World Cup Final!

Throughout the tournament expectation and excitement had been growing and growing. On the day of the final we had to travel about thirty kilometres from our base to the stadium and already there was that sense of frenzy. People wouldn't let us through, they wanted to see us, to touch us. The closer we got to the stadium, the more frenetic things seemed to get.

We were nervous, of course. But I still think the match that made us most nervous was the very first one of the tournament, against Hungary. I remember

César's words to us the night before that game. He was an excellent motivator, inspirational. 'You are nervous,' he said, 'but the important thing is that you don't move. Stay in bed. Don't get up, even if you can't sleep. Don't do anything. Lie down, rest, just stay lying on the bed, even if you're awake. If you can't sleep, don't worry, just remember the players from the other team can't sleep either.' Usually once on the pitch one continues to feel the nerves for a few minutes, then the football starts and one can focus. I remember against Hungary the nerves just carried on. They didn't go away. We were thirty minutes in and still the butterflies ruled; it took us at least as long as that to remember it was a football match and we had to just get over our feelings and play. And we went 1–0 down before pulling through with two goals.

It had barely been a month since that evening before our first match, yet it felt like an age. And here we were now, for the final, and again this nervousness. The atmosphere was tense, very tense. The stadium was completely packed, with the expectations of the whole nation in that crowd. And once again César's motivational words before the game were inspiring. I don't remember them in detail (though I do recall him asking us to think about our families, the people, everyone we were doing this for) but his exact words are in a sense irrelevant. The main thing is he transmitted to us the confidence and the belief that we could do it. We were so close, just one more little effort and we were there.

As the national anthems were played, as *our* national anthem was being played, so many things raced through our minds. Knowing we were one step away from glory, for example, but we still had ninety minutes to get through. Knowing we were almost caressing the cup, but that those ninety minutes were going to be difficult; and knowing at the same time that we probably should be thinking about something else, because if you think too much about the ninety minutes that are coming you are going to tie yourself up in your own nerves. And of course this all gets mixed up with more personal thoughts. I was thinking a lot about Silvia, my father, my mother and my brothers. Friends and some close relatives were there and many others were watching on TV in Córdoba; I was thinking about them all, imagining what it was like for them. And all the time a very defined thought was overriding all others: who was going to be marking me? What would I have to do on the pitch? Too much to hold in one head all at the same time, all these thoughts and emotions zooming around while we stood lined up and the anthem was played and the ticker-tape showered down.

The ticker-tape tradition is well established in

Argentina, but during the World Cup it became a kind of ritual: much more of the stuff was being used than in regular club matches. People throwing scrap paper before, during and after the World Cup was always something that went on – they still do it now – but the day of the final, now that I do remember. It was spectacular. The River Plate stadium, completely full, the crowd, all of them Argentina fans of course, the ticker-tape appearing from every corner, like a white cloud.

All that was very inspiring. Over time, as I watched the footage, I started to remember more and realize just how special it was. But at that moment we were totally and absolutely consumed by the football part of the occasion. I don't think, for example, we ever commented, 'Wow, look at the ticker-tape!' If you look at the faces of the players lined up you can see we were all so focused, almost to the point of being unable to enjoy the moment. I certainly didn't enjoy it at all at the time. I still have a feeling that I didn't really live the experience. The bus ride from José C. Paz to the stadium, for example, and the people surrounding the bus and showing their affection, cheering us . . . it's almost as if we didn't see it. It was all going on outside the windows but we were somewhere else, consumed by the match that was coming.

Kick-off was delayed by another one of those minor incidents which later led to rumours and misunderstandings, and not many people know it was me who initiated it. Basically, every Argentinian player shook hands with the Dutch players and handed over a little flag of friendship. These things are always a bit distracting and one goes along the line as if on automatic pilot: you shake each and every hand without giving it much thought. As I was about to shake one hand, I noticed something hard. Very hard. My immediate thought was 'he can't play with that', so I mentioned it to Passarella. 'He's got some sort of cast on his arm,' I said. Daniel and César leapt up to complain. I mean, it's one of those things. The Dutch should really have requested permission before the match. You can't come out on the pitch with a cast on your arm. And this was a long one, from the wrist to just below the elbow. And it was really hard, which poses a risk of injury for all players on the pitch. Anyone who got whacked by that would know about it.

It was so close to kick-off, the tension was mounting, and Daniel was making an absolute scene. In the end they put some sort of padding around Renee van der Kerkhof's cast, to soften the blow, I guess, if he hit someone with it. But the palaver delayed the start by many minutes and over the years it became a huge deal, more 'evidence' that Argentina had used tricks to put the Dutch off. At the point of bringing the cast to Daniel's attention I'd thought nothing of it. I simply reacted to something that was a potential problem, then carried on trying to concentrate on the game at hand. When I heard how much of a discussion was taking place, how Daniel and César were insisting and the Dutch were defending their decision, I was shocked. If I had known the fuss that would have ensued I would have kept my mouth shut. Really, come on, let's play! But I honestly reacted spontaneously. I just felt the cast was dangerous and mentioned it.

Eventually the match started and we were finally able to embark upon those last ninety minutes. Would it be glory or defeat? Despite our confidence, we couldn't be complacent, because the Dutch were a very good team. They weren't exactly the same squad from 1974, though. That mind-blowing, life-changing, revolutionary Dutch side had changed. Cruyff wasn't playing, for instance. He was the undisputed number one so we benefited from his absence. It's impossible to know what would have happened if he'd been there. And his absence is another one of those rumours that has changed and changed over time, suggestions that it was politically motivated going hand in hand with more gossipy tales involving women and angry wives, including a more recent version of a kidnap. I'm more inclined to believe the version that says Cruyff didn't play for personal reasons. That's just my opinion.

But even without Cruyff a number of the Dutch players were finalists from 1974 and it was a side that knew perfectly well what it was doing. They knew how to move on the pitch and they had been playing together for a long time. A dangerous adversary indeed.

10

As Long As You Can Take It

I had been doubtful as a starter. I was still in a lot of
pain from the injury I'd picked up against Brazil. I
could take painkiller injections which would allow me
to play but we had been very careful not to overdo them
in training prior to the final because you risk a delay to
recovery by forcing the injury before it's healed. So in
the days immediately before the final, César had many
doubts. On the one hand he was keen to allow me a full
recovery, on the other he couldn't settle on his team.
The ghost squad was beating us too often in training –
César never liked it when the reserves beat the first
team.

The day before the final he said to me, 'Osvaldo,
you're going to play.'

If it had been any other match I wouldn't have
played. But César needed to decide on the line-up and

he asked me to play. Now the problem was should I play the practice match as well the day before? I wouldn't feel any pain with the anaesthetic, but it could mean that the injury got worse. In the end I played fifteen minutes of the practice match, and I could see how César's soul returned to his body.

I started with Argentina in the final. The doctor had said to me that I should play 'as long as you can take it'. I made it almost seventy minutes, I think, at which point I was substituted and Omar Larrosa came on for me. Watching it on video later I can see I was almost limping as I left the pitch.

The first half was warlike. Very tough, a lot of fouls, a lot of interruptions to the fluidity of play. But we dominated. Mario scored, as it turned out from a move I'd started, but although I'm often interviewed about this I don't remember it as anything out of the ordinary. I had the ball and did what I had to, which was basically run forward and find the space for Luque or Mario. And, well, I managed it, and it was a goal. I never thought, 'OK, I've got the ball, this could end in a goal' – all moves can end in a goal. One doesn't think like that on the pitch. It was just a move, like any other.

The goal was pure joy. Not because I was involved in the play, that's irrelevant. The important thing was being 1–0 up in the final, which meant the World Cup was that bit closer. The celebration of a goal like that becomes special because of its significance, and the setting; but still there was no sense of enjoyment. Even now I couldn't say I *enjoyed* the 1978 World Cup, or the final.

In the second half, Holland dominated. They scored and they were better than us. When Rob Rensenbrink hit the post in the last minute I was already on the bench. I saw it almost in slow motion: the ball bounced, bounced again, it was going in, it was going to be a goal. That was it, goodbye Argentina, goodbye World Cup. For all we talk about tactics, technique, psychological preparation and all that, for all we try to understand the game, in reality it is ruled by unexplainable and impossible-to-prepare-for laws. That ball was going into the goal, but, as I watched, it deviated from its course. Perhaps it was a tiny bit of grass, but something just altered the ball's route a fraction and it hit the post. A few blades of grass in the end are maybe what defines everything. There is a lot I don't remember about that day, but that instant . . . that silence . . . and then phew, the total relief in the stadium when it hit the wood-work. That I remember.

Extra time. Again César gave us one of his motivational discourses, and again I don't recall his exact words. Profe Pizarotti had them recorded. It became a legendary speech: 'We are one step away from glory.' He went on to emphasize that we should remember who we were playing for: our family, our friends, our people. What I remember more vividly is that those of us who were on the bench sprang up and helped the others get ready, with stretches, handing out drinks and the like. We did our bit and encouraged those who had to play on. And in the final thirty minutes I think Argentina were the superior team.

When we finally won the cup I think rather than elation the overwhelming sensation was relief. That's it, *cumplimos* – we've done it. Yes, that was the number one emotion: before joy, ecstasy or elation I felt relief, that we had done what we set out to do.

From then on I felt like I was in another world, watching what was happening to me like it was a film. Like I was being shown a film in which I was the protagonist. I don't actually remember anything at all. The hugs, the embraces, the tears – nothing. I can tell you about it, of course, partly because I've seen it so many times since and partly because I was there, but the details did not imprint themselves on me.

I do know that it wasn't easy getting out of there. The streets were inundated with people and the traffic was at a complete standstill. Everyone had gone mad; they were out singing, cheering and celebrating. We had to go to the Hotel Plaza for a big reception, and the new challenge for the squad was how in the world were we going to get there?

I remember three of us – Norberto Alonso, Ricky and me – were leaving the stadium to do our thing first. I wanted to get home, where Silvia was waiting for me. So the three of us were smuggled out of the stadium in a police car. We had to hide because if the people in the streets saw us we knew we'd never make it.

I got home, sat around for a bit, then had to address the problem of how to get back into the centre of town to the Hotel Plaza. I decided to go to the local police station and explain the situation – and it was absolute mayhem there too. I was in there for ages, signing autographs and talking to people, even the ones in jail. I also had to go and meet the *comisario*, the senior officer in the district. After that I was once again driven in a police car as far as possible, but even a police car couldn't get close to the hotel so they stopped an ambulance, and we did the last stretch in the back of that.

From the hotel we all went our separate ways. To this day we are all in touch, see each other, have dinners together and so on. But that night we all went off to our own lives.

Back in Córdoba I spent quite some time living that same sense of triumph I had felt at the police station.

For ages I couldn't pay for anything anywhere in the city. Everybody clapped when I walked in. We were heroes.

It was a lot to process, but by then I was very clear on one thing: I wanted to play in Europe. I was thinking about how best to make the move when the president of Huracán rang and said there was a man from England who wanted to meet me.

I travelled to Buenos Aires and walked into the Sheraton where I was introduced to this man from England.

His name was Keith Burkinshaw.

11

The Move

As I remember it Keith, who had a translator with him, just looked at me. He hardly said anything. He just looked at me.

After the World Cup there was a lot of speculation about me going to play in Europe. I had made it clear that was what I wanted, but the press were going one step further and airing rumours about transfers. And not just about me, Daniel Passarella and Daniel Bertoni too (in fact all three of us left Argentina after the World Cup, Passarella and Bertoni going to Italy). Most of the rumours involved Spain, Italy, maybe France, but mostly Spain. I was getting calls as well but I wasn't really taking them. In all the post-World Cup euphoria everybody was ringing so I don't think it can have been easy to get hold of me. But of course when the president of Huracán got in touch I took his call.

'Osvaldo, they want you in England.'

England! I knew little about English domestic football. Internationally maybe, individual players – Kevin Keegan, their number one at the time, Trevor Brooking, Peter Shilton; a bit about Liverpool perhaps. In those days we didn't have the TV coverage we have nowadays, we saw only snippets now and then, so my knowledge of English club football was limited. As for Tottenham, I had never even heard of them.

During the meeting at the Sheraton I asked a few questions but I think it was a bit of a dialogue between deaf people. As I said, I just remember Keith watching me, and the bottom line was that the offer was on the table. Tottenham wanted to buy me.

I don't know exactly how, but Keith was persuaded that buying two players made more sense than buying one. He had been advised that acclimatization would be easier for two than for one, and Ricky Villa's name had come up, partly because we had shared a room throughout the World Cup, I think. So suddenly we had to get hold of Ricky and see what he said.

He was in his home town, Roque Pérez, where he still lives now. He always says it's where he would have lived all his life if football hadn't taken him off to distant shores. Ricky made his way to Buenos Aires and we met with Keith again.

The deal was good – I finalized it all myself. Today the idea of an international footballer representing himself in such a deal is unthinkable, but I had never had an agent, never have had, in fact. A well-known football impresario of the time had put the deal together but it fell upon me to agree my terms, and as it turned out I did Ricky's as well. We were on exactly the same pay, same length of contract, same everything.

The money wasn't spectacular but it was considerably more than we were getting in Argentina – an important difference, but the money wasn't the incentive. Europe was where all professional players wanted to play; it still is. And culturally, the continent fascinated us. I felt ready for the challenge, and Silvia was keen to go too. We had never considered England, but once we learned Tottenham was a London team we agreed to give it a try. Convincing Ricky took a bit longer, but his wife Cristina was more open-minded, and in the end he went along with it.

Ricky and I flew over to London for a weekend and signed, then went straight back to Argentina. A fortnight later we packed and joined Tottenham for pre-season in Holland, which is where we were incorporated into the Spurs squad.

12

The Island

At first, everything was a shock to us. We were, it seemed, the first foreign players to come to the English league, although we didn't know that when we arrived. A Chilean by the name of George Robledo had played for Newcastle about twenty-five years earlier but he had lived in England all his life and played his entire career here. Soon after we arrived two Dutch players, Arnold Muhren and Frans Thijssen, signed for Ipswich, which was then a club doing very well under manager Bobby Robson; and the Yugoslavian player Ivan Golac went to Southampton. But when Ricky and I joined Spurs all the players were British. No Italians, no French, nothing.

We were hailed as superstars – after all, we had just won the World Cup – and we attracted crowds. You have to remember TV wasn't what it is today so if you wanted to see someone play you had to go to live games. But even though there was a sort of frenzy centred on us – SPURS SCOOP THE WORLD ran one headline – and a lot of excitement particularly among the Spurs fans, there were voices of dissent. Gordon Taylor, of the Professional Footballers Association (PFA), the most powerful institution of its kind in the world, said we were coming to take the jobs of English players. Over time Ricky and I joined the PFA and Gordon himself became an ardent supporter and defender of our rights, but at the beginning there was opposition, and not just from him but from all corners, it sometimes seemed. Even some Members of Parliament voiced concern about our arrival.

I think all processes of change start off like that. The first thing that has to shift is the cultural preconception. And our coming to England was, in a sense, revolutionary. There were voices of opposition to our playing here, yes, but the country as a whole seemed well disposed towards us and received us very well. Slowly, this led to change.

It may not be so obvious now, but in the late 1970s England was much more insular. And so was its football. Great Britain was an island in every sense of the word, in terms of its food, its customs, even its sport. I remember we used to play on Saturdays and then

Sundays were so empty. There was nothing going on. Not even the pubs were open. Sometimes we forgot to buy something, a staple food like bread, and then it was Sunday and nothing would be open – no way of getting any food!

Moreover, the Empire's colonial mentality still prevailed. There was the issue of racism to be faced. There were hardly any black players in Division One, for example. Viv Anderson was the first black player to play for England and they used to boo him. All that has changed so much now, but when we arrived the novelty factor for the fans was huge. I can't say Ricky and I noticed all this, or rather that we let it distract us with regard to our football. Certainly it has to be acknowledged that our team-mates at Tottenham were amazing from the start. They knew all they needed to know about us: we had won the World Cup. The English respect a medal. More so than other nationalities, I think.

Still, in football terms it was very different to what we were used to. The mentality back then was that the English way was the best way to play. Bobby Charlton was the man most English football fans identified with. The FA coaching guru Charles Hughes even used to say that Brazil didn't know how to play football, that they were mistaken! I had a run-in with Hughes when I was training to be a manager, but that was many years later.

So Ricky and I basically spent the first few months, the first year even, watching the ball speed through the air – the famous 'long ball'. There were whole matches where we didn't get a touch. We were very surprised by this: they really didn't play football like we did.

I found it much easier to adapt than Ricky did. We had a translator to start with, and Keith would talk to me and I would explain to Ricky; but whereas I found the will to acclimatize and learn – perhaps aided by my analytical problem-solving approach – Ricky struggled. He was much more of an intuitive player, more like Mario Kempes. He could either play brilliantly or appallingly, but he couldn't analyse or dissect his performance.

I watched *Match of the Day* a lot. I used to love watching it. And I strived to learn English. All these things, I think, made it easier for me. And on the pitch I managed to learn the English ways. It wasn't easy: the ball often didn't pass through the midfield at all. But I found a way and by the end of my first year at Tottenham I was the club's footballer of the year.

Although I ended that first season on a high, we also had our fair share of hardship, not least the 7–0 defeat by Liverpool. I did not know this until I arrived, but Tottenham had only just been promoted back to the

First Division. Liverpool were the best team around and that match at Anfield showed what a different class they were compared to us. I think it was only from the second season on that things started to shift. Sometimes we played amazingly but often we let in stupid goals. It took time to consolidate ourselves as a team.

Football was so different in England back then. When you look at it now, the most visible change is in the game's finances. The Premiership has become the richest league in the world, without a doubt. When Ricky and I came over all the club owners were English; now this country is a melting pot of world money and talent. Perhaps the pendulum has swung too far in the opposite direction. I think not qualifying for the 2008 European Championship was a big blow for England, and it's worth looking at why this is happening to a nation with such passion and tradition in football. There are voices which point the finger at the number of foreign players in the Premiership but I don't think that's the whole answer, though it could be part of it.

A top division like today's was unimaginable in the late 1970s. Even England being part of the European Union was inconceivable. Unaware of what the future would be like, and oblivious to the fact that we were pioneers, in a sense, of a completely new way in English football, Ricky and I just got our heads down and tried to adapt to our new lives.

The club was very supportive. They didn't just throw us out on our own to cope, they really looked after us. There was a secretary who would drop in on Cristina and Silvia, we had an English teacher, we were even given identical houses right next to each other. Everything one of us had, the other had too: it was Ricky and Ossie, Ossie and Ricky, as if we were almost just one being. Everywhere one of us went, so did the other. We were very good friends already but in England we became more than that, more like brothers, more like family. We are godparents to each other's children. We never took two cars to training, it was always, 'Yours or mine?'

But identical twins we were not. Over time we made friends with different people, for example. The main difference was in character and style. Ricky always says it's very difficult to find someone who is one way in their private life and then completely different on the pitch. Maybe he's right. He is intuitive, emotional and spontaneous. He found England both different and difficult. I, on the other hand, fell in love with the place.

The work culture here is fantastic. I have since had the chance to work all over the world and England would be my first choice every time. Silvia and I and our two sons – Pablo, who was born in 1975 in Córdoba, and Fede, who was born in 1978, two months after the World Cup – are settled here now. I was here and living with Ricky and Cristina when Fede was born. We were in Manchester the night before a game against City, a Friday in September, when I got the phone call. Two weeks later Silvia came over with the whole family, including Juana (who used to work for my parents-in-law in Córdoba but who moved with us to Buenos Aires to help look after Pablo, and who has been with us ever since), and we are all still here. My first grandchildren were born last year and they are English: Pablo and his wife Aimee had a little girl and Fede and his wife Sarah had twins. A new generation of Ardiles, born in London.

I think the crucial thing is not that we were the first transatlantic foreign signings to English club football but rather the fact that we were the first foreign players to win. What started to shift the culture, in the main, was simply the fact that we succeeded. If we had failed, perhaps everything would have turned out differently, or at least taken more time.

We didn't stop to think about all these factors, though; as football men we concentrated on the game. But with hindsight I can see now the changes over the last thirty years in English football and it's clear that our impact on Tottenham and the success we had as a club helped forge the way. It wasn't long before other clubs felt a foreign player might add something to their squad, and I would argue that players from the likes of Ipswich's Muhren and Thijssen to stars such as Cantona, Bergkamp, Klinsmann, Zola, Henry and beyond have been huge influences on domestic football in this country.

When we first arrived, however, it was not a foregone conclusion that this was how our careers would pan out. In fact it was touch and go; we would have to see how things went. Many thought we wouldn't survive our first winter. How would we adapt to the climate and the food, never mind the football?

13

Feeling at Home

Our first match in Spurs colours was on 19 August 1978 against Nottingham Forest, at the City Ground. We had done pre-season and played in Holland, we'd also played in Ireland, but this was the first match of the season proper and it was our first in England. An important clash, too: Brian Clough's side were the reigning First Division champions (and would go on that season to win the European Cup). And we had just come up from the Second Division. Something I remember very vividly is that about twenty thousand people were left outside the stadium because it was sold out.

We didn't have that much of a clue about our opponents. Ricky had no idea, though I had a sense of who Brian Clough was – he was on TV all the time – and some of the club's background had been explained to me. We drew 1–1 with a Ricky goal. It was a good goal too, not as spectacular as his famous Wembley FA Cup Final one but a fine strike nonetheless. And he scored it against Peter Shilton. Peter was super-famous; he was the England goalie. For the thousands of Spurs fans who had come to see the champions against the club that had bought two World Cup winners it was such a triumph. The press thought it was marvellous, this team just up from the Second Division, playing away, drawing against Nottingham Forest – it was all praise, for us, for the club, for the transformation.

But we soon came down to earth with a bang. The first home game we played, four days later against Aston Villa, we lost 4–1. Three days after that, again at White Hart Lane, we drew with Chelsea, 2–2. And our fourth game was that hammering we received at the hands of Liverpool. It was as if that first game against Forest had been a sort of mirage. It was a message for us: the real test had started and we had better get on with the changes.

The feeling after the 7–0 defeat at Anfield was horrible. Luckily Ricky and I didn't understand much so from that point of view we were quite protected. We had no detailed idea what the press were saying, or what criticisms were being dished out by the manager, so we didn't have as bad a time as the other players. But we spoke on the phone with friends and family in Argentina and they all said they'd read that we were coming back the next day, that we were being sent home! That must have been what the newspapers here were saying, though we didn't actually have a clue where they got that from back home. I had to reassure them all that we were staying at Tottenham.

But the blow, tough as it was, helped us a lot. It gave us all, as a club, the knowledge of where we were at, truly, of how much work would be needed just to survive that season. After those early encounters we started afresh, with renewed conviction, and we ended that 1978–79 season mid-table without too many problems, which was a considerable achievement.

I also remember the very first derby we played. It was at White Hart Lane, against Arsenal, a couple of days before Christmas, and they beat us 5–0. They played so much better than us on the day. At that time Arsenal had a very competitive team under Terry Neill, a side that included the likes of Liam Brady (who scored a spectacular goal that day), Graham Rix and David O'Leary (a lot of them are friends of mine now, incredibly enough). But then I remember another match later when we beat them easily. That's just how football changes.

When I was playing for Tottenham the Arsenal–Spurs

Left: Schooldays in Córdoba. Here I am on the left with my youngest brother Miguel.

Above: I grew up playing football as often as I could; the picture on the right shows me in the stripes of Instituto.

Left: Good with my hands too! I was also a table tennis champion.

My wedding to Silvia in Córdoba. Through the connections of her father, in his military uniform here, the cathedral was full of people I hardly knew even though I was already famous as a footballer.

Above: The Instituto team with me second from the right in the back row. In the centre of the front row is Mario Kempes.

Below: Scoring for Huracán against San Lorenzo in March 1976. We were the best team in Argentina at the time.

Above: 25 June 1978. The moment every footballer dreams about: Argentina win the World Cup.

Below: In the dressing-room after the final. I'm in the centre with the manager César Luis Menotti on my right, and the captain Daniel Passarella right behind me.

Above: Keith Burkinshaw came all the way to Buenos Aires to sign Ricky and me.

Below: After the transfer, we were surrounded by journalists everywhere we went.

Above: Silvia and the boys, Pablo (left) and a very young Fede (right) flew in to England soon after the move.

Below: Golf has become a big part of my life, although this photo with Ricky was a little bit staged! I am proud that my good friend from Córdoba, Angel Cabrera, has won the US Open and the Masters.

Above and right: I love the sun, and so does Silvia, but England is our home.

Above and left: With my father Arturo and my nephews Emiliano and Mauricio, and (*left*) with my niece Maria Laura.

Above: *The Escape to Victory* team: with Ardiles, Caine, Pelé, and Moore!

Right: With my mother Blanca.

Below: The family settled in England. Both Pablo (left) and Fede (right) made me a grandfather in 2009!

rivalry was so strong. We couldn't even wear red. The passions between those two clubs . . . we couldn't put on a red tie or drive a red car. I knew what to expect from a derby – every player in the world knows what a local derby is like – but Arsenal–Spurs was a notch higher than anything I'd experienced. The north London derby was, well, *the* match of the season, incredibly important.

As the months passed, the team started solidifying, acquiring a shape. The most famous Tottenham side for me, the '81 side, was in fact a team that had started to be put together and take shape way before then. The two forwards were Garth Crooks and Steve Archibald, and in the midfield Tony Galvin was on the left (he was really a winger) and Glenn Hoddle on the right. Ricky was *libre*, free to play where he wanted, and then there was me, a little bit further back. I was the most defensive out of all of us. I could play in Ricky's position, in Glenn's, in Tony's – I could play anywhere. Keith Burkinshaw had tried out many variations; he had tried me in all those positions, and under Keith I always played. Sometimes he took a player out and tried another but I always played, here or there. One time he tried me a little bit further back and things started to work much better, so from then on I guess I sacrificed myself a little for the team's sake because the role was much more defensive than how I preferred to play.

At Huracán I had played further forward, as a number ten, and that was the position I liked the most. I tucked in and worked hard, but I was totally free. In the position found for me at Tottenham I felt much more inhibited because basically if I lost the ball there was no one behind me. So I started playing much more defensively. I realized that if I went on the attack, unless the move ended in a goal or the ball going out of play, we were vulnerable to the counter-attack. I could not leave my team exposed like that so I started to be much more cautious about going forward. This naturally meant that I did not score as many goals as I would have liked.

I don't like talking about my goals. Then again, among the few I did score, some were particularly satisfying. Against Manchester United, for example. I always loved playing at Old Trafford. After White Hart Lane there were other grounds where I loved to play, and Old Trafford was my favourite.

It's an FA Cup tie, a replay, and after ninety minutes it's goalless. Milija Aleksic, our goalkeeper, jumps for a ball against Joe Jordan, the great number nine for Manchester United, and falls with his teeth in his hand. There's blood everywhere. He's really badly injured, he's hurt his knee as well in the fall, and there's no way he can go on playing. We can't substitute him because you're only allowed one per match so for extra time we have no goalkeeper. And who goes in goal? Glenn Hoddle. We're playing at Old Trafford with all the pressure that signifies – fifty, sixty thousand fans – and Glenn Hoddle is in the Spurs goal. Which also means we don't have Glenn Hoddle on the pitch playing football for us.

It's still 0–0 after the first half of extra time. For the final fifteen minutes Manchester United's eleven players are all inside the area, all defending. It's one of those typical cup ties, everyone at the back. We're all exhausted, having almost played out a very intense match. Then, in the last minute of extra time – minute 119 – Ricky gets the ball on the left, passes two or three players and is at an angle to the goal. I'm positioned just to his right so Ricky gives me the ball and I trap it. I have a fraction of a second to decide what to do with it. I just haven't got the energy to whack it in so I decide to try to aim at an angle, to slot it in at the edge of the goal.

Pum! In it went.

As I said, I'm not one to relive my goals, or moves, but certain events inevitably stay with you. That goal is a little bit . . . it's entered Tottenham folklore, if you like.

During that first season we could have wondered what we were doing, playing in the dark, in the mud, losing 5–0, 7–0 . . . we're world champions, for goodness' sake! But we never thought about things like that. We enjoyed the competitive levels. The pitches were generally much better than in Argentina. It was a spectacular adventure for us. We were invited to all sorts of things. We were fêted.

Communication was always a problem, though. I was invited once to be guest of honour at a dinner at the Dorchester. It was an event for six hundred people, and I went with Ricky. The tickets were paid for – quite a lot of money – and we arrived late. That happened all the time, but we never realized. Anyway, at this dinner were all the Miss Worlds and Princess Anne, and all the men were in bow-ties. We were the only ones not wearing bow-ties. That happened to us fairly regularly too. Sometimes Silvia might be wearing boots and Cristina might be in trousers – not gala attire, put it that way. Sometimes the mix-up would be the other way round: we'd get our dinner jackets on and it would be an event in a pub.

In terms of football everything was much easier; the hardest things were off the pitch. But we travelled all over England, to Windsor, Oxford, Cambridge, and we explored London – Madame Tussaud's, Buckingham

Palace – and we relished it. We knew England better than the English players. And as we began to understand more of the language we began to make the most of the theatre, film, the arts. It was a gradual process, but we were soon enjoying life to the full.

14

El Enganche

A Spanish speaker remarked to me recently that it was always a struggle to translate the word *enganche*.

'For me too,' I replied honestly.

Enganche is basically the word we use in Argentina for the role of the traditional number ten – Ricky Villa, in a nutshell. A thinking midfielder, if you like, with a free role. When we first arrived in England the game here had nothing like it. If I was pushed for an English model I'd have to say Paul Gascoigne.

Ricky found the role impossible to start with, what with the long balls hardly passing through the midfield. He would ask for the ball but the defenders wouldn't give it to him. It's just not how the game was played in England, and Ricky really struggled. Eventually a sort of role was generated behind Crooks and Archibald, a sort of *enganche*, but initially Ricky was quite literally lost on the pitch.

The lack of a position equivalent to *enganche* in English football was one of many cultural differences in the approach to the game. We also have what we call the *gambeta*, for example, a term used in Argentina to mean 'dribble'. But it's not just the act of dribbling, it means dribbling *past* your rival. In Argentina, where there is such an extreme cult of individualism, the *gambeta* holds a particularly important place in the game's values. You can have an elaborate move between two or three players that ends in a fantastic goal, but in Argentina a move that is totally individual, like Diego's second goal against England in the 1986 World Cup or Ricky's second goal in the 1981 FA Cup Final replay, will always be preferred. Those examples are *gambetas* taken to their maximum potential.

The *gambeta* may be an Argentinian term but it's not exclusively an Argentinian concept, of course. In Argentina, where we sometimes think we've invented everything, we think we invented the *gambeta*. I'm not so sure. I'm much more of the opinion that the English invented football – and I have enormous respect for the English game and the industry of its players. As I've said, I've found this country a brilliant place to work in. But in those early days we were a little bit shell-shocked, totally groomed as we had been by *our* way of playing football, *la nuestra* – again, a term used in Argentinian folklore to somehow appropriate the game and the best way of playing it. It certainly became clear when we arrived that there was another way of playing football and it was the way it was being played on this island.

The English didn't know much about us either. Nobby Stiles was one of the few people I met who had been to Argentina, and he was full of stories about all the problems he'd had over there. Stiles was, of course, present at the 1966 World Cup quarter-final when the Argentina captain Antonio Rattín refused to leave the Wembley field after being sent off. I personally think the concept of 'cheating Argies' stemmed from there. But there wasn't much crossover, and I think as much as we were subjected to a huge culture shock when we first arrived, our coming here also shook the island mentality.

The technical level in England was very good. Outstanding, in fact. But I've mentioned this before, and it's something I keep returning to – the difference between excellence in technique and good football, between doing some things well and being a good player. Shooting well, heading the ball well, that's all fine. But a player who can do those things competently, even brilliantly, isn't necessarily the best player. This is an area in which I think England has serious problems. This sort of player is exactly the kind England has trouble producing.

The best players in England in the 1970s were Kevin Keegan and Kenny Dalglish – outstanding, but totally English in style (or rather British!). And then there are English players who were or are distinctive, a bit different – Jimmy Greaves, Paul Gascoigne, Wayne Rooney. Those players have always been few and far between in England, and when they emerge everyone falls in love with them.

In my days at Spurs, the epitome of the non-English English player was Glenn Hoddle. Hoddle had made his way up from Tottenham's youth side. He wasn't a typically English player at all. Over time I started to understand why the fans thought of him as a god, though for me that is too strong a word. He had remarkable talents which I noticed as soon as I joined the team, but in the late 1970s he wasn't yet the legend he would become. He hadn't even been playing in the first team for long: he was ever so young. But before long it seemed there were three South Americans in the team.

I think Glenn wasn't far from Maradona as a player. Perhaps Diego surpasses him a little in terms of pace, but otherwise Glenn is up there with him. He's as close to an *enganche* as there has ever been in England.

The other crucial man on our side was Steve Perryman, to my mind the best captain Tottenham have ever had. He was very welcoming and made us feel integrated and part of a team. He recently told a TV crew that when we first arrived he was more in awe of Ricky: his first impression was that Ricky was the better player of the two of us, because of his very South American style, I guess, the dribbles and touches. Steve said that such a precise touch 'in such a big fella' surprised him. They expected him to be a rough tackler but in fact he was a delicate player – beauty rather than violence.

Steve, a captain on and off the pitch, was open-minded about our arrival and also open to looking at football in a different way. He appreciated the efforts we made to blend in, to adapt, and reciprocated with the same effort. He understood my vision of the game, the way I was used to playing and the potential for change I was willing to bring to the pitch. He started to understand what we were doing and soon began to play a bit more like us, in tune with us. Then there were four South Americans in the side.

We definitely adapted to English football, but the Tottenham players were also influenced by our style. Before long we were playing a game that was a mixture of English and South American. Really, really lovely stuff – *lindo*. Much more passing, beautiful moves, intelligent playmaking.

We still needed some more players to become a very good side, and in 1980 Garth Crooks joined us. One reason that he signed for Tottenham, he said, was that they had two World Cup winners in the team, and that was unique at any English football club at the time. One of the major attractions, he continued, was that he'd be playing and training alongside genuine world-class players. A couple of others – Graham Roberts and Paul Miller – joined the club that year as well, with the specific intention of strengthening the side defensively, and then the team started to become powerful. The jigsaw was complete.

By the 1981–82 season we were on top of our game. It was our best year football-wise, the culmination of a steady improvement since we first arrived. We contended the Cup Winners' Cup during that campaign and reached the final of the Milk Cup. And we retained the FA Cup, against QPR.

In the Cup Winners' Cup semi-final we faced Barcelona. Those two legs were hard-fought games, and we just didn't make it. I played in both matches. In fact, I think I played every match in 1982, apart from the FA Cup Final because I'd already left the club.

The Milk Cup Final in March was great because we were up against the same Liverpool team that had beaten us 7–0 just a couple of months after Ricky and I arrived in England. Apparently back then there had been talk about 'Ardiles not being very good under that kind of pressure'. I'm not 100 per cent sure what was said because, either through the folly of youth, a lack of grasp of the language or a deep unconscious desire to suppress any difficulty, I didn't even register the criticism at the time. Maybe it was better that way. When we met Liverpool at Wembley in 1982 we were 1–0 up until the final three minutes when the European champions equalized and went on to win it in extra time.

We'd gelled as a group and this amazing side had emerged. I'm sure other clubs, watching Spurs, started to think 'perhaps it wouldn't be such a bad idea to have one or two foreign players in the squad'. The next season many clubs had at least one overseas signing, and so it continued, right to the extreme situation we have today. But I think it's clearly the case that the Premier League, which is today the number one league in the world, would not be anywhere as good as it is if you took out all the foreign players, in spite of the problems this may be causing for the national side.

Without a clue about the historic effect they would

have on the industry, I think those were without a doubt the best footballing years of my life. Playing with that team in those days was special. My overriding memory is laughing with Glenn, on the pitch. We just enjoyed it so much! I think the secret of it was the playing of beautiful passing football while at the same time retaining the efficiency necessary to get results – a huge accomplishment, and football at its best.

15

Ossie's Dream

I had always wanted to play at Wembley. All over the world Wembley is considered the cathedral of football – at least the old Wembley was. The Olympic Stadium in Munich and the Maracanã in Rio de Janeiro are also stadiums which as a professional player you want to play in, but for me Wembley was special. I had always been fascinated by the place and it had always been my dream to run out on to its turf.

I was very aware that there were only two ways in which a player could do this: by representing his country in an international or with a club that gets to a cup final. And in those days at least I'd bet that if you had taken any player in England and asked him to choose what trophy he would rather win in a given season, he'd have answered the FA Cup. It was the most coveted piece of silverware.

We played the semi-final in 1981 against Wolves, an incredible encounter which we won after a replay at Highbury, with Ricky scoring a stunning goal. And suddenly there we were on the brink of one of the biggest achievements in football, preparing for the FA Cup Final.

It was a huge deal. Everything was completely geared towards a triumph – the press, the marketing, even the song . . .

It was a tradition back then – I don't know if it still is – that teams that got to the final did a song. I don't know why this particular one became so famous; I think it even got to the top of the charts. Chas and Dave wrote it and it was centred around this idea that it was my dream to go to Wembley and win the FA Cup.

The song was therefore a 'true song', in the sense that I had always wanted to play at Wembley. It was, in a way, a mission of mine. Argentina had played a friendly there in May 1980 but I'd already left on tour to Saudi Arabia with Tottenham and Menotti was trying a young player in my place, Juan Alberto Barbas, so I hadn't played. So reaching the FA Cup Final in 1981 was indeed a dream come true.

I am by nature a rather shy and reserved man, and when I was told there was a line in the song which I would have to sing solo I was like, 'No, no, no and no.'

One thing that was guaranteed to make me feel uneasy was the idea of singing on my own on a record that would be released to the general public.

I didn't know until we went to record it that I was still expected to sing a line on my own: 'In the Cup for Totting-ham.' That's how I said it, because that's how I thought you said it. The 'h' in 'ham' – I thought you had to pronounce it. We never pronounce an 'h' in Spanish but in English, as far as I could tell, you did. Totten-*h*am. The other players always teased me about that.

As I said, I didn't want to sing solo, or even say a single word, but I came under a lot of pressure – from my 'partners in crime' – and eventually I did it.

Nowadays a lot of footballers do things like record songs and bring out CDs but it was never the case that I was interested in that type of thing. I went along with it because it was an FA Cup Final tradition, and the whole squad was doing it. And then, when it topped the charts and we went on *Top of the Pops* . . . John Lennon, eat your heart out.

I must say I didn't like it when we were doing it, I didn't like it when it was released, and I didn't like it after that either. Now I've come to appreciate it more. Perhaps it's a sign of how time can change a man that I've in fact grown rather fond of the song; I can now detect an enjoyment in the recording of it that was hidden for years. My fellow players tried everything to get me to relax enough to say the line – gave me drinks, insisted gently, talked to me – but I was adamant that we were a team and we had to sing it as a team. I would actually have said anything to get myself out of doing the solo. But in the end I was persuaded and it became the most famous line of the song. It represents a wonderful time in my life and my career.

My most serious concern remained the football, however. I felt the spotlight on me: my knees were trembling as the day approached and suddenly 'the road to Wembley' wasn't so much a jingle or a joke recording, more like my biggest footballing dream approaching.

Just before the first match there was a TV link-up to Buenos Aires – the very first live broadcast of an English club football match in Argentina. Our families had been gathered in a TV studio over there and we were chatting to them from a studio in London. It was unprecedented, an indication, if another were needed, of how big a deal this was, of how massive our achievement in reaching Wembley was.

In the final Ricky played badly. So, so badly. He was like that – he could have an off day for no discernible reason and that was that. Keith Burkinshaw substituted him – he had to – and Ricky left the pitch. That famous walk, all alone. He was furious and hurt and went straight off to the dressing room, which he now admits was one expression of his Latin temperament too far. We talked about it a lot afterwards. He asked me 'Was I really playing that badly?' and I had to nod with my lips pursed.

Ricky was very angry with Keith for taking him off. Keith was also very upset about the incident but he decided to give Ricky another chance and started him in the midweek replay. 'He wasn't happy about his game,' Keith commented, 'I wasn't happy about it. But I had to make a decision.' I think it said a lot about Keith's open-mindedness and faith in us, actually, his persistence in trying to understand Ricky's game and his relentless quest to find a position on the pitch for him. The second match would turn out to be a well-deserved reward for what was ultimately a pretty big gamble. Keith had good players he could have chosen instead of Ricky. In the end he started, and his superb performance that night was such a contrast to his display the previous game.

So what had changed? Absolutely nothing. When we talk about it now we still can't find an explanation. Ricky could be so good at times, Maradona would have been proud to be considered of the same calibre. At other times ... let's say you had trouble believing he was a professional. Sometimes I wanted to throttle him – how could he have no idea about what affected his game? But that was how he was: a truly special player who found it impossible to analyse his own game.

Just six minutes into the game Ricky scored a goal that was easy and of little significance apart from being the opening goal in an FA Cup Final. Except that in my opinion it is the goal that changed Ricky's life.

I say the goal was easy because the ball was bouncing almost on its own in front of an open goal. But the way things were at the time, if he had missed this sitter, if the ball had mysteriously deviated and gone out, Ricky would have felt so different. Instead, the way the ball went in filled him with confidence. I cannot emphasize enough how important confidence is in football. I repeat it a lot, this word, because I think it is fundamental. Often a mediocre player with a lot of confidence is more of an asset than a Maradona lacking in self-belief. A first goal generates confidence for the team as well, but on this particular night I believe that early goal is what boosted Ricardo Villa to have the match he ended up having. It was the enabler.

Originally we had both signed identical contracts for three years. They were coming to an end in the summer of 1981 and I had been offered another three years on very good terms; Ricky, who'd had a more tempestuous relationship with Keith and who'd found it much trickier to adapt in every way, had been offered a lesser deal, just one year on the same money.

And then, of course, Ricky, full of confidence and driven perhaps by a need to show everyone watching live back home that he could do better than the fiasco he had shown them the previous match, driven by his own dream and desire to prove himself a worthy player, passed one, passed two, passed three . . . a *gambeta* if ever there was an example to illustrate the term. I honestly think it was one of the most beautiful goals I've ever seen in my life. It was certainly momentous for Ricky. He was a World Cup winner but he always says he doesn't feel he really played enough to 'win' the World Cup. But this FA Cup win at Wembley, this was truly his.

And for all I had felt this would be my final, I am to this day so proud and delighted that it turned out the way it did. We didn't know then how legendary the match and Ricky's goal would become over time, but we were aware that we were the first true foreigners to play on Wembley turf at club level. My long-held dream had come true.

16

Escape to Victory

Immediately after we won the FA Cup, just three or four days later, the film *Escape to Victory* premiered in London. It was a huge gala event with Michael Caine and Sylvester Stallone, and the production team invited the entire Tottenham squad. We were *the* team at the time. So all my real-life team-mates and onscreen team-mates were there.

It was the first time I'd seen the film. I'd taken part in the shoot but I had no sense of what they would take out, what they would leave in, how things changed after the editing process. So it was a surprise for me to see myself up on that giant screen. I was dying of embarrassment, of course, as you can imagine, watching it with all my professional colleagues around me.

We'd made the film the year before, around June 1980. The shoot was timed so that all the players who were still active could make it. Pelé and Bobby Moore were no longer playing but a lot of us were, including me and the Ipswich players John Wark and Russell Osman. It was a Hollywood movie but with some English input. From a marketing point of view the producers had been looking for an Argentinian to complement the stature of Bobby and Pelé, who were legends. They'd got in touch with me through the club and I thought it would be fun. It was unusual in those days for footballers to be involved in a film.

The producers had some ideas about how the football scenes should play, in the sense that everything had been choreographed, but they were unconvincing – in a lot of football films the football is ugly. Bobby and Pelé convinced them that they should just shoot us playing and then choose the best bits: the scissor-kicks, the flicks, all the showy stuff. So they agreed.

Some parts were staged, rehearsed and so on, but I scored a goal that wasn't staged at all. Yes, it happened. I actually scored. And it followed one of the best bits of playmaking I think I've ever done in my life.

Escape to Victory was basically a war movie, and we trained in Hungary in a concentration camp, an actual concentration camp. We played against a Hungarian team that represented the German guards side. They were professionals, though, and they were good. The footwear we used were authentic World War Two boots – heavy, old, dark – but there was this one move where I passed one of their players, then another, then a third, maybe about five altogether, and the ball was getting away from me close to the line but I just managed to shoot with my right foot and it hit the crossbar, bounced on to the post and went in. The director was overjoyed and he turned to me and said, 'Ossie, the camera didn't get it all so can you do it again, please?'

It was one of the best moves of my life. You can't do those again.

Sylvester Stallone played our goalkeeper, and the climax of the film required him to save a penalty, which is when we all escape. Stallone knew which way the penalty shot was going to go – remember, for the film he must save it. The captain of the 'German' team was also a footballer but he was American – one of us, so to speak. So the scene was scripted like that: this guy had to shoot, Stallone had to save, we all celebrated, and amid the confusion we all escaped.

Stallone couldn't do it. I think it wasn't until the seventeenth take that he managed to save the penalty. Whatever the number of takes, we were standing around for so long that when he actually made the save all the players – Bobby, Pelé, me, all of us – were going 'What are you doing tonight?' and generally chatting, so nobody celebrated the save. Nobody even noticed it, but there was a big camera behind the goal that did. So the director shouted 'Cut, cut, cut! No good!' and we had to do it again – another seventeen times. I think it is literally take number thirty-something that appears in the film.

The film was based on a true story, or partly on a true story (it also hyped things up a bit). Concentration camp prisoners against the guards – it happened. I found it an incredible experience, and to this day there are places I visit where people still know me more because of the film than the World Cup or my contribution to football, probably because of the flick – I can honestly say that unlike Stallone I only needed one take. Incidentally, Pelé's wonderful overhead kick – the goal that drew the match – also only needed one take! I still get asked to perform the 'Ardiles flick' from time to time; sadly my knees aren't up to it, although I have to say it's not a particularly difficult one. The film was big at the time. It is still regularly shown on TV during the Christmas season.

We spent a whole month in Hungary, which was a communist country at the time. There were only a handful of five-star hotels and we took over one of them. I remember we had a bit of money every day for expenses and it was almost impossible to spend it –

there was so little to do. Every night we ended up in one of the very few top restaurants in Budapest. And then we would come back to the hotel and stay up very late, the actors and the football men hanging out together. Michael Caine was always with us. He loved football and he wanted to hear stories and chat about the sport, never about films.

We worked hard and trained hard. We went in early in the morning and kept going until five or six in the afternoon. But it was nothing like a football training camp, nothing like one. I was amazed by how long everything took. The lighting, make-up, this and that. For someone like me who knew nothing about film it was a surprise to see how much time you had on your hands doing absolutely nothing. We played chess a lot. Then for the few days when scenes around the penalty kick were being filmed they filled the stadium with extras, so all those people had to be fed and clothed, tables had to be laid out . . . We didn't eat with the extras, but we did eat with the director, who was no less a figure than John Huston, not to mention Stallone and co.

I had read a lot about World War Two, with respect to international law particularly. The concentration camp we were in was real. The barracks were authentic, the beds laid out. It had been touched up by the production team but it looked genuine. I was pretty shocked by it. Obviously we were making a film and it wasn't like going to visit a museum, but it did give me a strong sense of the conditions those people lived in. It was cold in the mornings in June, so in the winter it must have been bitter. Just more evidence of the stupidity of war. But I don't want to intellectualize the film because it was light and commercial. It wouldn't be right to make out that it had some agenda to show the unfairness of war, or the role of football in war. It was purely a commercial film.

I enjoyed the experience, though. Spending one month in Budapest allowed me to get to know Bobby Moore; we became friends. Bobby was a real, real gentleman – always willing to listen and always giving the correct advice. I am particularly honoured to have become friends with him. When one comes across people like Bobby, Pat Jennings or Alan Ball – in other words, rare gems – one must truly treasure them. Filming also gave me a strong sense of 'make believe'. Football has something of that, but not on the same scale as film. In film you stage scenes, you rehearse them. There's little room for the spontaneous. Football is life itself. Why is it so popular? Because it contains and gives vent to all the passions, ugly and beautiful. It is about solidarity and selfishness. It is a little bit of everything.

17

In the Eye of the Storm

The season following the FA Cup Final victory, 1981–82, was easily our best time – mine, Ricky's and Tottenham's. The team had found its sense of balance, things seemed to work out by themselves; all we had to do was enjoy playing. On top of our performance in the three cup competitions we challenged Liverpool for the league title and finished the season in fourth place.

I recall that period of my life as one of the best. Everything went so smoothly, so well. I remember thinking to myself, 'Things can't be this easy. Life isn't like this. Something's going to happen.' I think we all feel that sometimes, when everything's apparently going so well, that something's got to go wrong. I was thinking in terms of football, maybe an injury. I never imagined war would break out between the two countries that mattered so much to me, my two countries, my birthplace and my home.

Having said that, I must confess that there were two things uppermost in my mind about England and Argentina when I first moved to England. One was Alf Ramsey's remarks from the 1966 World Cup about us being 'animals', which I guess embedded the whole notion of 'cheating Argies' in the English psyche. The other was the Falklands, or rather the Malvinas as they are known in Argentina.

Growing up in Argentina, we have a concept of the South Atlantic map and that the islands on that map belong to us. I knew all about that, as any Argentinian would. But the last thing I expected to hear on the news on 2 April 1982 was that Argentinian forces had invaded.

We were playing a match the following day, against Leicester in the semi-finals of the FA Cup at Villa Park, and when we got there we were completely hounded by the press. But it wasn't the sports press, they weren't football hacks, they were news journalists.

We won the match 2–0 and it was my last match with Spurs in that spell at the club. It was quite amazing to hear the fans chanting 'Argentina! Argentina!' around the stadium. There was even a banner saying something like 'Argentina, you keep the Falklands and we'll keep Ardiles'. Quite something.

Many people think I left because of the war, but that wasn't the case at all. I was due to join the Argentina squad for preparation for the World Cup in Spain: Menotti had requested the players a month beforehand. It had already been agreed with Keith Burkinshaw; I was going to leave for Argentina that weekend anyway; the invasion of the islands simply coincided with a plan that was already set in stone. Ricky, who wasn't in Argentina's squad, stayed in England, and was here for the FA Cup Final – again!

He didn't play, as it turned out – a good example of how whenever football and politics mix, football is always the loser. The conflict had escalated into full-scale combat by the day of the final, 27 May, and the political pressures on Keith were sufficient that he felt unsure about playing Ricky. In the end I think he told Ricky to decide, and Ricky didn't play. Part of the reason was apparently because royalty gave out the medals at Wembley. Princess Anne was going to be handing over the cup, and should Tottenham win it was deemed inappropriate that a member of the royal family should give a medal to an Argentinian when the two countries were at war. So Ricky didn't play, and I think that's very sad.

I was back in Argentina and the final wasn't shown on TV there – obviously not. I spoke on the phone with friends in England and they kept me informed about what was happening in the match.

What we have to remember is that Margaret Thatcher, who had come to power in 1979, was very right-wing and had good relations with General Pinochet in Chile and the military junta in Argentina – so much so that Argentina bought several warships, commercial vessels and so on from England. I used to follow the political side of things, either reading about it in the papers or getting my information through the embassy. I always tried to make sure I was informed about what was going on generally in the world, but particularly so when it affected my two countries. So when war broke out my entire world collapsed. Truly. The country I was born in was in military confrontation with what had become my adoptive country. As the death toll rose through June I felt each loss, on both sides, deeply. Every casualty hurt.

It didn't start off as a full-blown war. At first it was just a 'conflict', and by the time the troops were deployed and the proper fighting began I was in Argentina with the rest of the squad. Over there we all thought we were winning the war. That was what the papers reported and that was what everyone believed. It was only when we arrived in Spain for the World Cup that we realized the extent of the misinformation we'd been fed, that the reality of the situation was in fact quite different. Typical Argentinian triumphalism, with all the propaganda. We were incredibly shocked when we got to Spain and heard a completely different story. A version made all the more believable when Argentina surrendered a few days later.

Meanwhile, the English tabloids had started running stories about me, claiming I'd said I wanted to go out and kill the English. Stuff that was grotesque and totally untrue. I was in Argentina when this started but I heard about all the barbarities that were being published. I was devastated.

But these things affected me a lot more later. During the World Cup I was coping. And I think I managed to play very well. I was a much better player than I had been in 1978, four years older, more mature and more experienced. I would say I was in my prime.

On paper we had an impressive squad: the 1978 World Cup winners plus Maradona and a couple of younger players who had come through, Ramón Díaz and Jorge Valdano. Those of us who had played in 1978 were now at the peak of our careers, still young but more experienced, still fit but more mature. And the young ones were outstanding: Valdano was already playing in Spain and on his way to Real Madrid, and Ramón Díaz was a brilliant player. It was, on paper, a great team, something of a dream team, and therefore subject to enormous expectation. Basically we were expected to win the World Cup again.

Individually we were a more talented squad than we had been in 1978, yet somehow, as a team we didn't quite cut it. Sometimes the team doesn't happen – I've learned this as a manager as well. Sometimes, for all the individual talent you gather together, the team doesn't play to the same tune, so to speak. And the 1982 Argentina didn't gel as a squad. We hadn't played qualifiers because as world champions we were through automatically, but we had all played a fair number of friendlies. In our matches prior to the World Cup we drew some, lost some and won some, but never managed to convince. I think we never succeeded in playing as a team. In my opinion, that's why we ended up doing so badly. The failure of 1982 was entirely down to this.

We lost our first match against Belgium and finished as runners-up in our group, and the way the tournament was set up, this meant we played in the second round in a group against Italy and Brazil. If we'd won our first match we probably would have faced only one of those two teams.

The Italy game was first, a very tough match. A special match, I think, as it prompted a change in the rules of football, mostly because of the way Diego was marked – it was foul, foul, foul. Claudio Gentile was marking him man to man and he was relentless. Diego was practically unable to play. After that match FIFA took measures to protect players a bit more.

We lost the game 2–1 so we had to beat Brazil to give ourselves a chance of going through to the semis. Brazil's squad in 1982 was outstanding, superior to their 1978 squad. Socrates, Zico, Falcão – unbelievable players. They beat us, and it was horrible. Diego was sent off after overreacting badly. He was angry, emotional ... and off the pitch. It was very sad, a terrible time for Argentina. The Malvinas, on the one hand, and the pearl we could have been as a football team on the other. There'd been an expectation that maybe we would distract from the sorrows of war ... but we tumbled out of the World Cup in a lamentable way.

We had a strong sense that we were better than that, that we should have done better. Maybe we were too full of ourselves, over-confident. It's hard to say what it was. After the Belgium match there had been an explosion of excellent football – we beat the Hungarians 4–1, which wasn't an easy thing to do, and I scored – but it wasn't enough. We left Spain hugely disappointed, weighed down by an awful sense of loss and defeat.

Nothing had changed in Menotti's philosophy, or in terms of our strategy and tactics, though this can never be a precise science. With Diego in the team the main objective was always to get the ball to him. In that sense it was easy. But he hadn't reckoned on being marked so closely, so viciously, and we hadn't counted on the team not gelling to such an extent.

Diego was already a very well-known player and his move to Barcelona was a done deal. I still shared a room with Mario Kempes, but César had asked me to keep Diego under my wing, so to speak, to talk to him and make sure I was with him a lot. I think the idea was that I was the serious one in the squad, and César hoped some of that seriousness would rub off on Diego.

Diego was receptive, very bright, and we spent quite a lot of time together. We had a free day just before the tournament started and Diego asked me the night before what I was planning to do. Our wives were in Spain and I told him I was going to drive down to a small village with Silvia and visit a church. 'I'm coming with you,' Diego announced. Now with Diego you never knew if what he said he was going to do one night was what he would do the next day, but in the morning he confirmed he was coming and we drove to pick up Silvia and Claudia, who would later become his wife. There was a car park where we were staying with a few cars at the team's disposal. They weren't intended for the players but they were there. We took a set of keys and drove off in one of them, knowing full well that if we'd asked for permission it would have been refused.

We all drove off to this small church in a remote village. When we got there the place was filled with eleven-, twelve- and thirteen-year-old children in their white robes taking their Holy Communion. Diego was already the number one player in the world, and I wasn't exactly anonymous, and as we walked into this church the whole place froze. The priest interrupted the mass, a little murmur started among the churchgoers, and then the priest asked if after the communion was over we could have our picture taken with the congregation.

In the meantime, back in the team camp they'd noticed that two of their main players were missing. Mayhem ensued, because the war was still ongoing at this point and there had been rumours in the Spanish press of plots to kidnap Argentinian players (though we were oblivious to this). And the two players who were missing weren't just any two: it was Diego Maradona and me, and my connections with England might make me a particular target. Security were alerted and a spectacular amount of searching took place until some-one said they'd heard us say we were going to church.

So the security guards, in full gear – dark glasses, uniforms, the lot – went down to the village and literally stormed the mass, found us and dragged us back to the hotel, along with the car we'd taken.

That's an example of the happy memories one gathers while playing football; it wasn't all despair and defeat. But the war, I think, symbolized a loss of innocence in a sense. We were, as people, very hurt when we learned the facts as opposed to what we had been told back home. We felt betrayed, cheated, lied to. We had, practically without exception, been convinced of Argentina's sovereignty and right to the islands, and were therefore supportive of our nation. I had a personal conflict of interest, but in no way did I doubt our right to the Malvinas.

In Argentina, General Galtieri, who was in charge of the junta, had taken some blows: the issue of 'the disappeared' was cropping up as something people heard about and talked about. He was losing power. The Malvinas was seen as a solution to remain in power – a quick fix. It never entered their minds, not even for one moment, that Thatcher would react the way she did. Suddenly they found themselves confronting England, and not just England but the Americans too, because the US were clearly supporting the English.

I only realized all of this much later. I look back now

and the escalation of the conflict, the planes flying off to Port Stanley, the *Belgrano* . . . on a personal level I identify it as a very dark period. And it strikes me as a silly war, if only in the sense that war is always a demonstration of man's inability to resolve conflict in a civilized way. And, like all wars, it was begun and its course was dictated by political powers.

In this case, on both sides there was a situation where the powers that be needed to regain popularity. In Argentina we had a corrupt, non-democratic government which had been in power for some time and could see its end was coming. It was coping at the time with internal problems, even an uprising. One solution was to invade the Malvinas as some sort of popular crusade. On the British side Margaret Thatcher was also losing support and, with her politician's hat on, she must have seen an opportunity: deploy two-thirds of Britain's substantial military power in a task force to the other side of the world and kick out the aggressors. Many agree that Britain's victory was a key factor in the Conservatives winning the 1983 election by a landslide.

I'm neither a diplomat nor a politician, and I have close ties to both countries, but personally I believe the islands should belong to Argentina, because of geographical and historical arguments: geographically because of their proximity to Argentina, and historically because they used to belong to Spain and were part of the Spanish territories which became Argentinian after our independence. Two hundred years ago the British, when the Empire ruled the waves, arrived on the islands and took them over. From then on there was a British base there. Anyone can see that if one goes to some islands and populates them with British people, several generations later those people will feel British and will want to stay British.

But just because my personal opinion is that the islands should belong to Argentina, that doesn't justify at all the invasion, or the war that ensued. And I would like to stress here my respect and admiration for all those who fought in it, all soldiers, both British and Argentinian. They of course only follow the orders issued by the political powers. Without doubt there were acts of heroism on both sides. I would want to pay my respects to all who lost loved ones, relatives, husbands, sons, fathers.

I think before the invasion Argentina was working along the right tracks, through discussions at the United Nations. A war was unnecessary. The way forward is always to discuss, negotiate, and stay on the side of peace.

* * *

After the World Cup I went home and was due to join Spurs for pre-season again, but the press hounding and the air of conflict remained. I thought I would be unable to return to play in England and suggested I should be transferred. Keith was adamant he would not accept that under any circumstances and simply told me to stay in Argentina for a while, take some time to recover.

I took his advice, and didn't come back for six months.

18

The Consequences of War

It's important to stress that during the World Cup we had concentrated totally on the football side of things and the war had absolutely nothing to do with our performance or our losses.

I played very well, for example, much better than in 1978 – on a personal level, I mean. But of course when one wins it's easier to be in the running for the label 'best midfielder in the world'; when you lose . . . well, nothing. That's it. You don't exist.

But the really difficult time for me came after the World Cup, after I realized I wouldn't be able to go back to England. A black part of my life. I felt so torn; I felt as if I couldn't open my mouth. It was a lose – lose situation for me. If I was asked why I liked England and I chose to say, for example, 'Well, the golf courses are great, and the people are polite and nice,' in Argentina they interpreted it as me sucking up to the enemy; similarly, if I was asked about Argentina and I said, 'Well, the meat is very tasty, and the people are fun and *simpático*,' the same thing happened on the other side.

There were stories in the press all the time. I was called a traitor, here in England too. The issue was firmly established in the media, unarguably on the agenda, and I couldn't shake it off. Until then I had felt somewhat invincible: people could say what they wanted and I would always reply playing football. That year I had been one of the contenders for Player of the Year. I was confident and my football was in its prime. But after the conflict I felt very low. I couldn't go back to England. Spurs offered to continue paying my wages, everything remained the same, but I still felt the urge to take time off.

Eventually Keith Burkinshaw reluctantly agreed that I should look for another club. There had been some offers from Italy and Spain but Keith said, 'No, no, we're not selling you, no way.' So it was agreed I would go on loan for a year. And that's when Paris Saint-Germain came in for me. I thought, 'Paris is nice.' And off I went on loan for a year.

My football there was lamentable. There's no other word for it. It makes me think about all that stuff I was telling you about Diego. Whatever happened in his life, no matter what was going on, once on the pitch he was in control. I wasn't like that. I couldn't shake off my depression. (It was extreme enough that when I did finally return to Tottenham they found a psychologist to work with me, a guy called John Syer. He wrote a book afterwards. But that was later.)

Keith continued to watch me and knew perfectly well that I was in a terrible state. He didn't have to ask me or tell me anything. He knew me inside out. All the time I was in Paris, playing dire football, his insistence on my return was like an echo. Even before I agreed to the Paris deal he urged me, right up to the last minute, 'Don't do it, you're making a big mistake.'

But even if I'd wanted to come back to England, I wasn't certain I'd even be allowed into the country. Right after the 1982 World Cup there'd been a problem with the work permit. Keith sent a secretary from the club, a man called Peter Day who is still a very good friend of mine, to the Home Office to see if they could somehow sort out the problem. All Argentinians had had their accounts in England frozen and suddenly we required an entry visa, which we hadn't needed before. Peter spent a week with me in Paris telling me he thought I should go back to England, at least for a few days. Sure enough, when I gave in and decided to go I didn't get the visa, so I wasn't allowed in.

'Goodbye, Tottenham,' I thought. 'Goodbye.'

But I didn't really want to come back because of the war. I thought I would feel bad about it sooner or later. I had this idea that I would walk down the street and feel uncomfortable. Ricky had stayed in England throughout the conflict and he was telling me it was fine, it was manageable. But I'm different. I'm more of a thinker. I often ask myself, why do I analyse things so much? Why do I ask myself so many questions? I knew I would be uncomfortable, in a deep sense.

So in my mind the Paris move was settled. I started practising French. But Silvia wanted to go back to London. Desperately. Pablo was seven so he was settled into school. Fede was younger, but still, our lives were in London. I knew lots of players who club-hopped and the family problems this caused were in some cases really quite serious. So the pressure to return was huge. It's not very stabilizing for family life to be moving all the time.

We returned to the British Consulate in France to see about the visa, which had become something of a drawn-out affair. I remember the consul refusing it, and me saying, 'But . . .' and him stopping me with the words, 'No buts, Mr Ardiles.' I remember that line so clearly. Someone suggested going back via Ireland, without passports, on a ferry. I just thought, again, 'Goodbye.'

A couple of months later there was a complete turn-around and I was finally given the visa. I went to watch a match at White Hart Lane and the wave of affection was so intense. I think that's when I decided to return.

Now don't get me wrong. We enjoyed Paris to the full. We had an amazing flat, spectacular, and a great car. The kids were at the international school. It was all good. Paris is a very beautiful city, you know. The main problem was the football. I couldn't believe I was capable of playing the game so badly. The ball would come to me, I would try to control it and it would just get away from me. I was thinking, 'What is this? What's going on here?' In the end I reached an agreement with PSG, who I think were delighted to let me go. I was playing because of my name, basically, but I was no good, so they happily released me.

In January 1983 I was back in England as a Spurs player. But I still didn't feel up to scratch. I was better in football terms, my game was much improved, no doubt about that. But in my head I wasn't OK. I wasn't well, and I felt a certain animosity, from people and from the press. I have to be honest and say that neither Ricky nor I ever had a problem on a personal level in terms of attacks or insults, and our team-mates were, as always, excellent in their attitudes towards us and the war. I can't say a word against them. That goes for everyone at the club, from the chairman to the kitman. Our fans, too, were brilliant. But when we played away and Ricky or I touched the ball, they'd boo us. Of course the war was still present as a theme. It was over, but still an issue. Before the war now and again when we got a touch of the ball we were booed on an away pitch, but Glenn Hoddle also got a fair bit of this sort of treatment – it's a normal thing for fans to do to throw you off your game. It's almost a compliment: you're good enough for them to bother. But now I felt the boos weren't so much to make us lose our concentration, they were hostile. I couldn't take it.

My head kept churning the Malvinas issue around all the time – not helped by the fact that it crept up all the time on the news on TV. Although some things did normalize over time, within myself I continued to feel bad.

Not least because there was a family connection with the war. I had a cousin who was a pilot in the air force and was shot down. My uncle spent a long time trying to locate his body, to find out what exactly happened. There was talk of an island where Argentinian prisoners of war were being held, a British island. My uncle came over to England to look into the matter, hoping, I suppose, that he would find my cousin alive. He went to the Ministry of Defence, and everywhere he went they were incredibly polite and treated him very well. It seemed that my cousin had been killed.

A long time after that – because immediately after the conflict no one was allowed to give out details of combats – my uncle got a letter from the British pilot who had struck down my cousin's plane. It was very respectful, its intention to communicate to my uncle all the circumstances of the strike, and confirm that there was no chance my cousin could have survived. The British pilot didn't express regret – obviously – but his respect for a fellow pilot was clear.

War wounds don't heal easily. It takes time. I had thought staying away from England was the solution for me, but for all the glamour of Paris I came to see that England had become home. My family and I had to come back.

19

If You Want to Make God Laugh, Tell Him Your Plans

The title of this chapter is one of my favourite lines. I think it applies particularly to football. One move, one detail, changes everything in a second. We have to be very conscious, very aware, that we are in the hands of God, Fate, whatever you want to call it – in the hands of the ball, if you like, and which way it will bounce (or not bounce).

We speak of football as the theatre of dreams for a reason. When I was a player – and now as a manager too, really – I often felt like an actor. An actor in a play, say, who plays the same role every night but whose performance can vary. Sometimes you're inspired and you do well, sometimes not so well. For both actors and footballers this can happen, and in this sense our professions are incredibly similar.

But maybe football is more drastic. In football there

are no rehearsals and no second chances. The possibility of a repeat performance doesn't exist. And the scoreline dictates everything. Football, for all its drama and theatricality, is in fact more grounded in reality. The course of destiny is affected by every performance and by all the circumstances that surround it.

The FA Cup Final in 1981, for example: it was programmed for us to win. Manchester City fans will read this and say, 'What?' I don't mean programmed in the sense of fixed or arranged, I mean given the context – a Manchester team against a London team; the 100th Cup; twenty years on from the Double; and maybe because of the film *Escape to Victory* as well – it felt like we would win.

After the win it became a little bit like the golden era of Tottenham, at least for those of a certain age. For older fans the golden time was under Bill Nicholson when they won the Double and the European Cup Winners' Cup – and that was bigger – but for younger fans the prime years of the club were when Ricky and I came over and Keith established the 'dream' side with the likes of Glenn Hoddle and Steve Perryman, and the crowning moment for that team was winning the FA Cup in 1981.

From then on we were established as one of the leading forces in English football, and from then on

Manchester City started to fall. It could easily have been the other way round, though: they could have won it and become a force to be reckoned with and we could have fizzled out.

When I first came to England I was planning to play only for three years and then I was intending to return to Argentina and finish my law studies, maybe in time become a judge. I told Ricky that was what I was going to do. Then, when that Tottenham side really took off, and amid the excitement and the pleasure – because when things are going well playing football is pure pleasure – I renewed my contract for another three years. I was still planning to leave football after that, but when the time came I just found it impossible to leave the game. This has happened to all the players I've known, all my Argentina team-mates and my Tottenham team-mates. It is an incredibly difficult thing to be in football and then not be in it any more. People stop asking you what you think about your club, about results; you get asked for your opinion less and less, maybe every other week, then once every couple of months, until eventually you become no more than a memory. It's like fading away until you cease to exist.

So, my original plan had been to quit after three years with Spurs, but I renewed for another three years, and after that difficult time in Paris I returned to England full of desire to play and with no plans to stop. But you never know when the trigger for change will be pressed, on the pitch or off it. In professional football, in fact in all elite sports, the risk of injury, the unpredictability of injury even, is a huge factor in that.

I had always been lucky. I had colleagues who had to be extremely careful with their diet, for instance. Ricky is a case in point: he couldn't eat a slice of cake without having to lose the weight the next day. I was the opposite: they were always trying to shove more food into me. At Tottenham they gave me chocolate on a daily basis. I like chocolate, so I felt lucky. I was small so I was always given more food. If I fancied two steaks for lunch, no problem, two steaks it was!

We didn't have nutritionists and dieticians and all the experts that abound today in football clubs. It's interesting how such details in football have changed. We wouldn't have dreamt of eating pasta before a match back then, and nowadays it's all pasta, pasta, pasta. I guess in those days the worry was that the sauce might cause a digestive upset. There's some irony, I suppose, in that being exactly what happened to the Spurs squad not so long ago, in one of London's best hotels, no less.

What I'm driving at is that so many tiny factors must

coexist for an outcome to be one thing instead of another.

For me, many aspects of the elite athlete's care and day-to-day existence came completely naturally. Running was easy. I guess I took it for granted. I notice such things only now that I can't do them any more. I couldn't run for the bus now, for instance, because of my knees and ankles – the natural wear and tear that's the price you pay for being a professional sportsman.

Over the course of my life, I have had seven knee operations and, including surgeries for hernias and so on, probably about ten major surgical interventions. They are all the result of playing top level football. In 2002 I had what is known as a complete knee replacement – this was the final intervention and I'm delighted with the results. The operation was a complete success. But I still feel the pain of hearing the doctor say, after the procedure was completed, that I really ought never to kick a ball again. To actually hear him say it! Fortunately, I was already fifty years old.

Ricky hadn't been as lucky as me. He had a career-threatening injury in the run-up to the 1981 FA Cup Final. In fact he had hardly played much before then and had needed surgery for a cruciate ligament injury, which is incredibly serious. At one point the club suggested he quit. There was an insurance sum payable if your career was cut short through injury and he was advised to take the money and cut his losses.

One of my fondest memories is when his wife Cristina went into labour with their first daughter, Maria Eugenia. Ricky's leg was completely out so he called me to drive them to the hospital. We piled into the car, with Ricky stretched out on the back seat because he couldn't bend his leg: his plaster cast stretched from his pelvis to his ankle. When we arrived he said to me 'Go with her!' because he knew it would take so long to get himself out of the car. So I ended up walking Cristina to the delivery room with people looking at me, thinking I was the dad-to-be! In the end he got there in time.

This amusing aside shows that you have to take whatever hand life deals you and make the most of it. But if he had done what seemed at one point the most sensible thing and taken the insurance money, the goal that turned out practically to define the rest of his life would never have been scored. A goal that also turned out to mark the beginning of a golden era for Tottenham.

People often think it started when Ricky and I first arrived, but I think it was in that third year – the one in which I would have stopped playing if my original plan had stood. That plan shifted as both circumstances beyond my control and my own desire to play also changed. I became increasingly aware that I wanted to play for as long as possible – until the bitter end, in fact.

Playing football is pure pleasure. Anyone who has played well understands this. Crowds of fifty, sixty thousand, millions watching on TV. Playing for Argentina was a huge honour, one of the best things in life, but also a big responsibility and pressure. The same with Tottenham. And you have to be very strong to stick with it. For no player is it simply a bed of roses. Football is like life itself: it's impossible for it always to be good; sometimes it can be incredibly cruel. Those who make it are those few who are mentally equipped to take the pressure. That's just how it is. Only those with the mental strength to endure all the stones and rocks that are hurled, to overcome the obstacles that appear along the way, survive.

And to accomplish this you must change. Change is very important. Change means adaptability. Flexibility. Another parallel between life and football. In life itself if you don't change – I don't mean the essence of who you are, which doesn't need to change – you won't grow. You have to permanently adapt to new situations. As a player, too, you have to adapt to whatever is happening on the pitch and off it. Those who make it to the top are those who are able to be flexible. Those who can't be like that crumble and die. Yes, adaptability is the key word, because change happens whether you want it to or not.

As a footballer I almost never had an argument with anyone. In some senses I think I was a bit like the dream player for any manager. I never had to be told what to do on the pitch, either; I was basically just told to get out there and play. In some ways I was a little bit like the manager on the pitch. I had a sound instinct for what to do in any given situation and was able to direct the others on the pitch too. The manager at Instituto when I first started playing top-division football, Humberto Merlo, was asked about me once and he said, 'Ardiles breathes football through every pore.' I liked that comment a great deal, I felt very flattered, but I had honestly believed there would be other things in my life. I had other interests, not least my law studies. I'd never thought of football as the be-all and end-all of my life.

And then, after I returned to London in 1983, after the incredibly difficult time I'd had in the aftermath of the war, I was struck by injury. It happened during a match against Manchester City at Maine Road. A ball was played to me by John Lacy, and David Cross, City's centre-forward, tried to tackle me. He barely scraped my fibula, but it resulted in a fissure – a long, narrow crack in the bone. It really wasn't that significant an injury, I simply should have rested, but we had a lot of important games coming and the recovery was rushed.

That's how all the problems started. I kept on playing before I was fully fit and got worse every time. In the end the injury kept me from playing regularly, fluidly, for almost three years. I would play, touch the ball or try to run, and I'd get injured again. I was never quite fit enough after that and started to spend more and more time on the bench, something that I was not used to, as I had only ever been on the bench on a handful of occasions, for specific reasons. And on those few occasions I hadn't found it at all easy. I even had to have a metal plate inserted in my leg, which I think was the trigger for other problems: I couldn't run very well, and that did my knees in; and later I had hernias, one bad one. I'm sure these were all consequences of the initial injury. It was a depressing period for me, because you see your team-mates running and jumping and you're on a stretcher.

Tottenham continued to progress, and in 1984 we won the UEFA Cup, but I didn't participate very much in the campaign. I did come on as a substitute in the final though, and it was from my pass that we scored the goal that sent the game to extra time. That game against Anderlecht was one of the great nights at White Hart Lane.

Most footballers, I think, have a defence mechanism which is essential for survival, because not playing affects your confidence, and if your confidence is diminished you will play less well every time. That's a fact. We see it all the time, in every team. A player is substituted and immediately feels bad. He thinks 'Why me?' and blames the manager. It's the manager's mistake, or the other players'. That mechanism is crucial for survival. It is bound up with self-preservation, and it has to be that way. I have used that defence myself as a player. We'd lose a match and I would try to find a way in which we didn't lose because of me – any way in which it was the other ten who lost, not me. There was always a lot of self-criticism after that, of course. The defence-mechanism response was simply the immediate reaction, one that is very important for confidence and self-belief, must-haves for a footballer: as I've said, I'd prefer a mediocre footballer full of confidence than a Maradona with no confidence. And there is such a thing as Maradona with no confidence. Diego has played badly. But his mechanism on such occasions was 'it wasn't me'; it was always someone else's fault for not giving him the ball, and so on.

This sort of response happens across all sports.

It's harder to blame someone or something else in individual sports such as tennis and boxing, but it happens nonetheless. I think the key is to strike a balance between whatever one's psyche needs to find confidence again, to claw back self-belief, and an ability to be self-critical, to learn from one's mistakes. A top-class athlete must be on a perpetual quest for self-improvement.

Amid the throes of what could have been the end of my career, peppered with a few appearances on the pitch which were enough to keep me feeling alive as a player, another unplanned change happened at Tottenham: the club became the first in England to become a plc and was listed on the Stock Exchange. It may seem bizarre to today's generation of football followers who live in a world where there's hardly any club which isn't a listed company, but back in the early 1980s it was a sign of the extent to which Spurs was in the middle of a revolution. At the time it was a big deal, both shocking and controversial.

Keith Burkinshaw, who is in my opinion not the best but the second best manager the club ever had (and it would be a close second to Bill Nicholson), and who had been such an influential and close ally since my arrival, decided to leave the club, mostly because he was so opposed to the commercially minded turn football seemed to be taking. His parting line, 'There used to be a football club here', has stayed with me.

There was no denying the fact that his decision marked the end of an era.

20

The Swansong

During the 1983–84 season I played maybe fifteen or twenty matches, and of those maybe three were in the UEFA Cup. I was so struck by injury that for the second leg of the final against Anderlecht, when Keith decided to put me on the bench, I remember thinking I wasn't even fit to be there. Steve Perryman was suspended, Glenn Hoddle wasn't available either, so Gary Mabbutt came into the team. Neither of us was fit – Mabbutt was probably 70 per cent and I was about 50 per cent – but Keith decided Mabbutt had to start and I should go on the bench.

The first leg was played in Belgium, and at my invitation my brother Miguel came over for that match. (He met the woman who would go on to become his wife on that trip, and he lives in London to this day.) We won the cup, on penalties, back at White Hart Lane. I handed my winners' medal to Steve Perryman. I didn't feel I should keep it. I gave it to Steve because I felt he deserved it more than me, having played every game bar the final (later, however, Tottenham very kindly gave me a replacement medal).

When that second spell with Tottenham began for me the squad was the same one I had left in May 1982. Even Ricky was still there. The problems started when I got injured and Glenn got injured (he had very serious problems with his Achilles tendon), and when Keith left, well, that clearly spelled the end of that period in Tottenham's history. From one point of view, maybe, it was necessary, but the commercial side of things started to become increasingly prominent. Tottenham had been a family club, to put it one way. Irving Scholar was the chairman then, and things started to change. Irving had serious run-ins with Keith. Basically, Keith always wanted the last word. Maybe that's how it should be – definitely from the football point of view that's how it should be. Keith felt he couldn't work at White Hart Lane the way he wanted to, and the UEFA Cup Final was his last match in charge. And yes, it was a shock, a great shock, for all of us. Keith had been the Spurs manager for nearly a decade.

When Keith left, Peter Shreeves, who had been Keith's assistant, took over as manager; John Pratt was

Peter's assistant so it was all in the family, all Tottenham, excellent. We knew Peter inside out and got on with him very well. Keith had been more of a manager, but Peter was clearly a coach. He loved beautiful football and always got involved in the kickabouts. He used to joke, 'Give me the ball – I'm the only one who knows how to play here!' He loved football. When he was appointed manager he said he wanted to build a team based around Glenn and me, even more so than it had been before. He called us both and told us that. But it was bad luck for Peter that Glenn and I both had serious injuries. The team suffered a lot and started to dismember – Steve Archibald, for example, left to join Barcelona – and in the end it cost Peter his job.

I think the principal problem was that when Glenn and I were in our prime, the team was constructed around us in a way that made sense. But our absences led to the team breaking up. In spite of winning the UEFA Cup in 1984, the level of our football had diminished from the sort of displays we put in regularly in 1981 and 1982. The idea was to try to recreate that team, but it just wasn't possible.

The more injury kept me out of the game, however, the more desperate I became to return. I was itching to play, in spite of my fears, and my feeling that my career was as good as over.

Carlos Bilardo had taken over as Argentina's manager by then. He was Menotti's antithesis, the most extreme symbol of the anti-football mentality of the sixties and seventies Menotti had come to replace. I was very identifiable with Menotti's philosophy and his view of football, so there was a sense that Bilardo was reluctant to include me in his squad because of this. My football was suffering during this time, but there was a period – after winning the UEFA Cup, and then intermittently in 1985, when again I didn't participate very much but the little I did was good – when I played well enough to put Bilardo under considerable pressure back in Argentina to include me in the squad for the Mexico World Cup.

During one of my trips to Buenos Aires I had a three-hour meeting with him, all about football. I think it was mostly pressure from *El Gráfico* and other areas of the press that forced this 'chat'. I'm pretty sure he was reluctant at first but he accepted it in the end and we discussed English football, Argentina's standing, everything you can imagine about the game. Bilardo was under a lot of pressure from all quarters to include me in the squad, but injury marked the end of my dream of playing in my third World Cup.

So I did what players do when their time is up, and in May, just a few weeks before the World Cup kicked off, my testimonial was held at White Hart Lane. I invited Diego Maradona to come and play for our side and he agreed – he wore the Tottenham shirt! Glenn Hoddle and Chris Waddle were also on our side. It was a great team. We played against Inter Milan, and Liam Brady played for them. It was a wonderful and moving occasion, even though I only played about ten minutes. I couldn't have endured a single moment more. That was it: I wasn't going to play again. Pablo and Fede came on to the pitch. They had never been there before, and they were on the turf with Diego and Glenn. I think it was pretty exciting for them.

After the match I invited all the players to Trumps, the nightclub. We stayed there until about four or five in the morning, then I said goodnight to everyone and thanked Diego especially: he doesn't really play charity matches or play for free but he was very keen on this occasion and had left Bilardo's training camp between two warm-up games. Bilardo was quite unhappy about it.

Then I went straight off to hospital to have surgery on a double hernia.

Dr Gillmore, who was taking care of me, came up to me the next day and said, 'You can run now.'

'Run?' I thought.

I had to admit I felt fine. More than fine – I felt great.

You can run now.

I thought he was crazy, but I started walking and everything felt right. Ten days later I felt terrific; I was running around comfortably. Before surgery I couldn't bear the pain, I couldn't manage the ball at all, I couldn't do anything. And now I was feeling great – on top form again!

We spoke about it at Tottenham and decided to give it one more go. David Pleat, the new manager of Tottenham, under Irving Scholar's insistence, agreed that I would go on a contract that would be renewed every month. So I spent the summer looking forward to another season in football. Which is why I think of it as a swansong, one last performance before you perish . . . My rebirth was coming.

Throughout the 1986 World Cup I worked as a commentator for the BBC, no less. I watched the England v. Argentina quarter-final in Spain. Now that is something I do remember clearly – the infamous 'Hand of God' goal. The first time I saw it, live, I didn't notice anything untoward. I don't think it was clear from the first camera angle, but someone did say 'Ooh, they're complaining', and when they showed the replay I looked more closely and saw that two of the English players remonstrating with the referee were Glenn Hoddle and Chris Waddle, my team-mates at

Tottenham. And if they were complaining it was because there was something to complain about – neither was a player to make a fuss over nothing.

On the second replay I noticed Diego's reaction to the goal: he looked at the linesman – another clue. I thought, 'There's definitely something going on here.' Was it offside? But that didn't seem to make sense either.

And then I started paying more attention to the replays, and yes, it was a handball. I don't think it's obvious from the first take but when you view it from different angles . . . well, it's obviously a handball.

Diego has come to England several times since, and especially around that time I was always with him when he came, always his local contact, if you like, his guide. We were very close. But it took years before he openly said, 'I scored with my hand.' The 'Hand of God' remark was witty, maybe, but ultimately neither an admission nor a denial.

At the time it was one of those incidents you never think will take on such momentous dimensions. More was made of it than was necessary on account of the Malvinas background to the match between the two countries. I know people have interpreted the entire performance as somehow being an act of revenge for the Malvinas. I think Diego himself has been quoted making reference to the fact. Which makes me want to state more than ever: let's not mix war and football. Whenever sport and politics come up against each other, sport is always the loser. It happened in the 1980 Olympics when the US refused to go to the Soviet Union, for example. And who or what came out worst affected? Sport. When the military tried to take advantage of the 1978 World Cup to utilize it for their political ends, what was affected? Football. Again.

This issue for me is hugely important. Football is one thing, politics is quite different.

Back in 1982 Diego was very patriotic, very national-istic, as were we all. We had all of us, practically without exception, felt unequivocal about the islands being part of our national territory. Over time some of us may have felt more or less betrayed and cheated by our own government, become more or less politically anti-war than we were beforehand. But our comments and opinions, as footballers, on any issue, be it social, political or whatever, are identical in weight to the comments and opinions of any other person. In this sense we are just citizens.

Football is a game, played on a pitch. It is about beat-ing your rival, but whoever that opponent happens to be and whatever non-sporting issues surround the encounter they must be kept totally separate from the game. To suggest that any of that game was in any way some sort of 'revenge' for the Malvinas is ridiculous, grotesque. Ask any of the people who lost a son, a loved one, in the conflict.

21

First Steps

The following season, 1986–87, was truly a miraculous one in my life. Because I wasn't ever going to play again, I'd literally hung my boots up, not just in my head. Then suddenly I wasn't just back, but back like in the good old days. It was a gift from life – the least likely thing to happen. I played my last match and then I was back with the ball at my feet, just like it was before. And it wasn't just me back on form, so was the team.

I think after the glory days of the early 1980s, and the Bill Nicholson era, of course, that season was the best in Tottenham's history. David Pleat had replaced Peter Shreeves as manager, and he put together a great team. Richard Gough joined us to strengthen the centre of defence. Chris Waddle was there. Glenn was also in his prime, and we were enjoying playing together again. Clive Allen was fully fit and scoring goals for fun. It was an excellent squad. We finished third in the league and got to the FA Cup Final, where we lost to Coventry. We shouldn't have lost but, well, that's football. That final – more specifically how we lost that final – is one of the most disappointing moments of my football career, because that team was exceptional. We were favourites but we just didn't perform well enough. It was a bitter day. Then again, for me personally, just to be an active member of an FA Cup Final squad was the best reward imaginable.

I had started out thinking I would quit at twenty-nine, then decided to stretch it a little until thirty-two, now here I was at thirty-five playing as well as I ever had. This was the time when I realized I would never be able to leave football. In fact I think now I never did. Football left me. I would have carried on and on. It's addictive, like a drug. It gets harder and harder to stop.

In 1987–88 we still had a great team, but then one of those bizarre incidents and its ensuing treatment by the press changed the course of things at White Hart Lane. I can recall playing somewhere like Manchester or Birmingham and cars driving by with people holding the front pages of the newspapers up to the window. David Pleat had been caught by the papers and he was sacked from his job. These things happen in football and in life and I'm not someone to go around judging anyone for how they choose to behave privately. But once the story was in the hands of the press he had to go.

The manager chosen to replace him was Terry Venables. He was at Barcelona and had about a month left there before he could take over so an interim manager was sought, which turned out to be me. I stayed on the same wages and the same contract, nothing was different, but I was the player/manager. Pleat's assistants had left with him, so I stepped in to fill a big hole, with Doug Livermore and Ray Clemence as my assistants.

I enjoyed the experience very much. I had always felt a bit like a manager on the pitch, with a vision of the game, thinking about everything that could happen, and I had a feeling that managing Tottenham was somehow my destiny. I relished that first taste.

When Terry arrived he had to build his own team and it was clear that the first person to leave should be me. I was too emblematic of the old regime. I also think, in all honesty, my football had begun to decline again. The injuries I'd suffered were taking their toll.

There was a particular match I played under Terry, in the second half of the season, when I got a very strong sense that I was no longer the player I used to be. I lacked pace and acceleration, and that really detracted from my game. Of course I was still able to do lots of things but I was no longer the player I had been.

It was clear Terry no longer wanted me in the squad. A possibility of going abroad cropped up around this time but I turned it down. Terry started not playing me – I was on the bench, basically. I understood that as a manager he had to take certain decisions in order to create his team, and leaving me out was the obvious one.

And then the idea of going to Blackburn came up, and it made sense. Steve Archibald had come back from Barcelona and was playing at Blackburn, who were then in the Second Division. There was about a month left of the season and the club was facing the play-offs for promotion. Archibald spoke to the manager at Blackburn, Don Mackay, and he asked Tottenham if I could go on loan for a month. So I played there for the last weeks of 1987–88.

We didn't go up to the First Division – Chelsea beat us in the play-offs (Chelsea, in the Second Division!) – and after the summer I didn't go back to Tottenham for the 1988–89 season. I was thinking about what to do, whether or not to leave football. In the end I went to QPR because the manager Jim Smith's assistant was Peter Shreeves, and he loved me. He spoke to Jim and I joined the team. (Later that year Jim took over at

Newcastle, and when he left I took over – you see the twists of life?)

During the year I was at Loftus Road I spent more time in the treatment room than on the pitch. Towards the end of the season, in March, I saw the ball coming and I tried to jump for it but my foot didn't have the necessary spring. I broke my left leg. That should clearly have been the absolute end of my playing career.

But I was addicted. I couldn't give up. Bizarrely, that early summer of 1989, while I was recovering from the break, I received an offer from Fort Lauderdale Strikers. The suggestion was a brief trial period playing soccer in the US during the European summer, so I thought, 'Why not?' Again, it was a way of staying in the game, and the contract was short. I wanted to know if I could carry on playing or not. I thought I might be able to continue playing in England. There was no football here for the summer recess and the US gave me the chance to see if I could still play. I was fit enough and good enough to play there: it wasn't a very high level of football. It was also a time when the furore of Pelé, Beckenbauer and co. had passed and the US was still struggling to revive its football industry.

We did very well and emerged as champions of the American Soccer League. I became champion of America! But I didn't play in the final because that same summer Swindon made me an offer I couldn't refuse: to become their player/manager. I took it.

The US contract had only a fortnight to go when I said yes to Swindon. The family had had a great time in the States – we visited Disneyland, and all our relatives from Argentina had come to stay – but football-wise I wanted to be in England. England was home, and I still think it's a perfect country to work in.

Swindon's offer was good. It would enable me to keep playing, which I was very keen to do, and also gave me a chance to learn the ropes of management, which was my future. Swindon was in the Second Division but it was a good club. The challenge for me was promotion, and there were some big clubs in the Second Division at the time, the likes of Newcastle and Leeds, all clubs with budgets ten times the size of ours.

Our first match of the 1989–90 campaign, against Sunderland, we lost 2–0. At home. I was trying to do everything – take the free-kicks, manage, everything – and I got everything wrong. I was shown a yellow card and I should have been sent off.

It was a fiasco, so for our next game, away at Oldham, I decided to put myself on the bench. We were winning 2–0, playing quite well, but they were putting a lot of pressure on us. I decided to bring myself on, thinking I might calm the situation a bit, keep the ball – slow down the game, basically. The match ended 2–2. That should have been an easy match for me. We were 2–0 up and I should have come on, taken the ball, and that should have been that. I realized then that it was over. That's when I thought, 'I'm never ever playing again in my life.'

And I never did.

22

Man On!

Thirty-one years have now passed since the Argentina World Cup, since I first started playing in England. When I look back on my experiences over those decades so many of the memories of games I featured in come and go. Other impressions, feelings of how it was, are stronger.

When I arrived with Ricky everything was a novelty. Football itself I didn't find particularly difficult, if I'm honest. I don't mean to repeat myself but I was short-listed in the top three players of the year both by the PFA and the Football Writers that first year at Tottenham, and I was one of the best three players in the whole of England, which is good evidence that I didn't have too many problems adjusting. Maybe the first month, the first couple of months, but no more than that. I found playing in England like a breath of new life. I loved playing here, even when the matches were tough.

People compare football then to football now a lot, and I would like to say this: nowadays it is unthinkable that a League One or even a Championship side can win the FA Cup. And this is despite the fact that, for the big clubs at least, the FA Cup no longer has the importance it had – so much so that Manchester United, when they played the semi-final against Everton in 2009, basically fielded their reserve team; a few years ago they didn't even take part. Nowadays, by the time we get to the semi-finals, it's almost always four clubs from the Premiership, and of those four three will be from the top four. Back then luck played a much more conspicuous role. If you played away at Cardiff or Swansea, for example, those matches were incredibly difficult, much harder than now. Why? Mainly because of the pitches. Now all the pitches are perfect so many elements of luck are out of the equation. All those long balls, crosses, centres, headers, big forwards who could score any minute – basically any club could cause you problems.

Finances are also a major factor. Now they say a team with no money can't win the Premiership or the Champions League, but three decades ago Nottingham Forest, a medium-sized club to put it generously (and currently in the Championship), won the European Cup twice in a row. So times have changed a lot. Nowadays the clubs that reach the Champions League Final are basically the same year-in year-out, the ones that have the most money: Manchester United, Barcelona, Chelsea, Real Madrid, etc.

Getting back to the state of the pitches, well, Wembley was the one and only. It was perfect. There were some stadiums that were inspiring places to go to – I always loved playing at Old Trafford, as I've mentioned – but the pitches were nowhere near as good as they are now. The ball could bounce any which way, and if you had to play a Second or Third Division side you could end up playing on pitches that left a lot to be desired. Nowadays they wouldn't be considered good enough for League Two even. Not to mention the fact that in winter the grass was replaced by mud. Slippery, wet mud.

When Ricky and I first arrived we had just come from playing in the World Cup so we had got used to superb pitches. But that was in the World Cup stadiums, all specially prepared. In our careers before then we played on poor-quality grounds as well, but with one difference: instead of mud we played on dry earth.

Quite simply, poor pitches make playing good football

harder. I would love to play today on these amazing surfaces on which the ball always bounces perfectly and you don't slip. Some of the surfaces I played on, when I was a boy especially, the only thing about them that was a 'pitch' was the name. That is, however, all very good training for ball control. When I got here, the pitches (when dry) were a little bit better than in Argentina. I guess that helped me get used to England.

It was easier for me than for Ricky. Ricky, as the *enganche*, was used to having the ball passed to him, but as I said, in England no one was used to passing the ball to the midfield, that wasn't what the game was about. You had to go out and look for it, fight for it and win it. I did that: I sought out the ball, fought for it, grabbed it. In those first few months I was involved in the thick of the action on the pitch. For every five touches I had Ricky had maybe one. His first two years were tough for him. He felt very frustrated. Basically he didn't have the ball at his feet enough to develop his game.

Talking of tough early years brings back more memories. When we first arrived in England there was a press furore. Most articles were favourable but there were also some strongly worded ones that were incredibly critical of us, of Keith Burkinshaw, of the club. I remember one in particular, a double-page spread headlined MERCENARIES. But at the time we didn't really read the papers because we didn't understand them. I think Ricky has probably not read them to this day!

Of course football generates very strong passions (I think there are two universal languages, football and music, and each creates very particular passions). The newspapers have to sell and they have to write about whoever is producing the headlines, and when they get the tiniest whiff of a story, a confrontation or a conflict, they're on to it immediately. That's what happened later on at Tottenham with Ray Clemence: it was all blown up by the press when in fact there was no conflict.

At the beginning we didn't understand much. Much? I mean we didn't understand anything. Nothing at all. We made do with sign language. We had a translator to start with but he was with us for seven days at most. We immediately developed all sorts of ways of making ourselves understood, a dictionary to hand at all times. I was very motivated, driven, determined to make myself understood and to understand what people were saying to me. I started to grasp very quickly whatever the player closest to me was saying.

One of the first things I learned was the expression 'Man on!' I soon realized that it meant someone behind me was trying to get the ball off me.

23

Hoddle, Waddle, Perryman . . .

I have to say I had the great luck to have played at Tottenham with some incredible players and characters. I can't name everyone, all I can say is each one was different and it was a real pleasure.

In 1978, the rest of the side was clearly a team that had just come up from the Second Division, and promoted from third place in the division as well. Tottenham was the strongest contender for relegation that season. The fact that we finished mid-table was a huge achievement. Aside from the fact that we started very badly – that 7–0 defeat at the hands of Liverpool and so on – within that squad there were players whose ability was remarkable. And of those, two grabbed my attention because they were so good: Glenn Hoddle and Steve Perryman.

Glenn was simply outstanding. It was a pleasure to

play with him. We were on the same wavelength. It was like knowing each other by heart. He was often criticized for not knowing how to defend, but I had no defensive problems with him, none at all. He was also accused of never tackling in his life. No, he didn't tackle because he didn't need to. But at that time in English football culture if you didn't tackle you were slighted. How could you have a player who didn't tackle, who was weak, who can't defend, and so on?

The thing about Glenn, though, was that his football intelligence was so great that even if he appeared not to be defending he was always somewhere on the pitch actually complying with his defensive mission. And with the ball at his feet Glenn could . . . well, there's a reason they called him God. He could put the ball wherever he wanted. And apart from all this, he knew how to play football, in the way I talked about before. He had a spectacular panoramic vision of what was going on all over the pitch. And his technique was superlative: as I said, wherever he needed the ball to land, he got it there.

There was always a healthy competition between us. Which of us was better? was a question always on people's lips. I never saw it that way because in fact we performed very different functions, but for Tottenham people there was always this competition between us. Glenn spoke to me a lot because he saw me as an older, more experienced, player. When I arrived in England I was in my mid-twenties and I'd just won the World Cup with my country; Glenn was very young, twenty or so, already a starter in the first team but really just emerging, his career only just beginning. So of course he liked talking with me about football a lot.

We spoke a lot, particularly when he returned from playing with England, because in those days the England team weren't used to winning every match they played, put it that way. They hadn't even made it to Argentina for the 1978 World Cup, and they only just scraped through in 1982. And back then every time England lost it was Glenn's fault. That simple. I remember a match – I'm almost sure it was against Bulgaria – when he scored a beautiful goal, and then yes, everyone spoke very highly of him. But when England lost the blame fell on him. As if the other ten hadn't played. As a result Glenn often used to come back from national duty devastated, and Steve Perryman and I would talk with him a lot and try to lift his spirits. When one plays for one's country the press dissect you, and Glenn was their constant target.

Steve Perryman was also technically outstanding; he too could do whatever he wanted with a ball. Less exquisitely, I would say, than Glenn – and he didn't have that creative streak Glenn had – but he was, not just as a captain but also as a player, Mr Reliable. They used to say that when Keith Burkinshaw picked his squad he wrote down Steve Perryman's name first, then chose another ten players. Steve always played, and he always played at a certain level or above. He might not always have been spectacular, but he was always on a good level, good and rising. So he was the one we all leaned on. It didn't matter where we played, whatever the circumstances, if things weren't looking good for us, Steve was the foundation rock.

Much later, in 1985, Chris Waddle joined us – another outstanding player. He had quite serious problems when he arrived at Tottenham because he was surrounded by big stars and big names. He arrived at the same time as Paul Allen, who also found it a bit difficult, but after a while they adapted, and Chris went on to play for England and for Marseille. He was a very skilful player.

Of the Tottenham players that were there in our first season, very few survived to our third year. It was clear that many changes needed to be made to the squad that had just come up from the Second Division. My great friend John Lacy also came to the club in 1978 – to this day he is my golf partner – and there were many more. Two very important additions were Steve Archibald and

Garth Crooks. They were the missing links because until they arrived, for all that we played a beautiful, skilful, eye-catching game, we were still lacking in terms of the end product. Those two provided us with that end product. They scored an impressive number of goals, the way Clive Allen did several years later (he scored forty-nine goals in one season). We played with just one striker in those days, who was fed the ball relentlessly from a midfield consisting of Chris Waddle, Glenn Hoddle, me and Tony Galvin. The number of goal opportunities we generated for Clive between us would have been a dream come true for any striker.

We called Tony 'The Russian' because he studied Russian. He had finished secondary school and had taken on Russian at university. Why? I'm sure even he doesn't know why. Which is typical of Tony as a person. Being in tertiary education, he was absolutely an exception to the norm. Completely. Both in England and in Argentina it is extremely rare to find a footballer who has gone on to study beyond the obligatory schooling. And having said that, the level of education an English player receives is superior to that of an Argentinian player because school in England is compulsory until the age of sixteen whereas in Argentina it is compulsory only until the age of twelve. That's without taking into account the fact that in Argentina a lot of players, even in the First Division, haven't even completed primary school. Over here that would be completely unthinkable, even illegal. It's still the case, however, that most footballers in both countries rarely finish secondary school. I think things are changing slowly, but I always felt a little bit like the odd one out, studying law. The English didn't understand it that much either, but there was always Tony, or 'The Russian' to us.

When I went to Swindon my assistant manager left for another club and Tony Galvin became my assistant. And when I moved on to Newcastle I took Tony with me, so we have a long history.

Another Spurs regular with whom I enjoyed a long and close relationship – in fact our families are close too – was Chris Hughton. He was an excellent footballer, and we played together for eight years at White Hart Lane. He became part of my 'kitchen' when I joined Tottenham as manager. He started coaching the reserves, and it was then that Steve Perryman and I realized he had enormous potential as a coach.

When I was playing and for whatever reason had to come off, the player who mostly took my place was Micky Hazard. I think the only player who had more pure talent than him was Glenn Hoddle. Micky really was exceptional. I took him to Swindon when I went there and brought him back to Tottenham when I returned to White Hart Lane as manager. That's how much I rated him; he was one of my favourite players.

But I think I learned an important lesson with him. In a sense it was like I wanted to change him. I could see his immense potential, yet he had some psychological limitation, something that prevented him from flying to the top. He was summoned to the England squad once. He didn't want to go. I practically forced him. He was looking for excuses and finally he spoke with me because we were incredibly close. I persuaded him and he went. Still, he hardly played for England in his entire career.

I'd always had this conviction, perhaps a bit of a romantic one, that it was possible to change a player. Later in my career, as a manager, I learned that one can change many things – you can make a player more intelligent from a tactical point of view, for example, and you can improve technique – but there's one thing you can never change and that's character. That's what let Micky down: he didn't have the competitive character needed to reach the absolute peak of football, even though his natural talent was clearly good enough.

24

The Fool on the Hill

I think in many ways Keith Burkinshaw and I are very similar. Like I said, that first time we met he practically didn't speak, and I don't think I spoke much. He's a typical Yorkshire man, honest and straight, a man of few words – *de pocas palabras*, as we say in Argentina. He never told me what to do or how to play football but he was always challenging me, teasing me: 'Let's see, world champion, how you handle this', that kind of thing. He had an incredibly dry sense of humour. He certainly spoke a lot more with me than with Ricky. I think Ricky and he must have exchanged a maximum of two or three sentences in all the time they worked together!

We're also similar in the sense that neither of us enjoys social situations; we tend to avoid lots of people. And we're both modest in the sense that we don't like being flattered or praised or congratulated. I think it makes us feel awkward.

Before matches I got nervous and never wanted to think about the game, so I would chat to the kitmen. Most of the team would go on the pitch before the match, but I didn't like to go out too soon: I thought running around would tire me out. I stayed behind in the dressing room, chatting and jumping a bit to warm up, trying to get my mind settled. And Keith was always there, teasing me, joking around, trying to motivate me.

The element of banter in a dressing room is a very important part of team building. It's a comforting, special thing. At the very beginning Ricky and I were at a loss, but the team as a whole were amazing because very soon the banter and the joking took off even with the language limitations. I joined in, though always at a level my language abilities allowed.

Practically every away game, on match day morning Keith would take us walking. Sometimes it was freezing. He would be at the front and the players behind. Sometimes these walks were incredibly long and many players protested. I always did. In a good-spirited way, of course: just gentle moans about being frozen, and tiring ourselves out before a game.

I remember one time, a Saturday morning some-where in the north of England, it was so cold and we were going uphill and I started to say, 'Keith! Keith! Beetleson! Beetleson!' And everyone, including Keith, was saying, 'What?' I put my index finger to my forehead, pointed at Keith, shouted '*Loco!*' and tried using sign language and gestures to get across the idea of a mountain or hill. 'What?' everyone kept saying, and then Steve Perryman, who was very quick, said, 'Do you mean "Fool on the Hill?"' Yes! We laughed so much. I think the very attempt to make a joke in a foreign language is often funnier than what might come out of your mouth if you spoke fluently.

As my English progressed, the level of my jokes adjusted. For quite some time my main gag was to exaggerate the fact that I didn't understand anything. I understood what was being said to me – perhaps not the exact words but certainly the gist of it – quite early on but I didn't always let on, I would just sit there making out I didn't understand anything, forcing the other guy to stand there and attempt to explain himself in more and more convoluted ways. The longer he took and the more he tried, the more I just stared blankly. So he would mime and do funnier stuff to get me to understand. And then Steve would realize what I was doing and we would all burst out laughing.

When I left Tottenham in 1982 I was replaced by Gary Mabbutt – in terms of my position, I mean, because in terms of style of play he was very different. Gary had a spectacular career. I remember when he first arrived at White Hart Lane. Spurs had bought him from Bristol Rovers as a gamble and paid very little money for him. He was clearly out of context among the top players at Tottenham but it's a testament to Gary's enormous capacity to learn that he came as a midfielder, ended up playing central defence, and was at the club for years, becoming captain and an emblematic player. When I was manager at Tottenham he was my captain. Gary played for England on several occasions and his career was outstanding. But if you'd seen him when he first came . . .

Another player I really should mention is John Pratt. John often tells the anecdote that he was on holiday when a friend phoned him and said, 'Tottenham have just signed two midfielders who just won the World Cup.' John is a very good friend now, but at the time he took it as direct competition: he was a midfielder, and us two coming along meant he feared he wouldn't play again. 'Forget it,' he thought when he got that phone call.

It was clearly the case that whenever we had a bad result, if John had played, Keith seemed to blame him. He never said so explicitly, but whenever the result was poor the next match John wouldn't play. Very simply our problems at the beginning were in defence, and John was more defensive than the rest of us put together, but Keith couldn't take Glenn or Ricky or me off so he would take John off. So he became the scapegoat.

John was an incredibly honest player; he always gave 100 per cent. Maybe the reason he didn't make it to a higher level in football – and in my opinion he should have made it to the top – was because he thought he could do absolutely everything. He had no mental limitations. If he took a corner and kicked the ball badly, the next corner he would go and take it again. And if it was another poor attempt you can imagine what the fans and everyone thought. But that was his character – incredibly honest. It was a real pleasure playing with him.

It was, as I keep saying, a pleasure to play with them all.

25

Staying in the Game

When a player stops playing football it is very traumatic. A complete shock. It's what you have done all your life, and suddenly it's over. It's hard from the point of view of other people's interest in you and in your opinions – you slowly become a memory. But it's also incredibly hard in terms of your own notion of self.

After being a player, becoming a manager is second best. A poor second best, but it means you're still in football. I went into management as a substitute for playing – in my case, I think this is clear. I've had many interests in my life but the adrenalin of football became essential. I delayed leaving the game as a player until I reached the very limit of what my body could take. And by my late thirties I finally had to accept that I would never leave football.

I found that as a manager I remained in a team. In

many ways you become the most important member of that team. You are certainly the most important before the match: you have to exude confidence yet keep the players relaxed. You are the most important at half-time, too: you have to understand both your own team and the opponent and draw your comments from what has happened, and you have to be able to communicate all this to your players in a useful way. And you are the most important after the match: you have to lift spirits or quash euphoria and gear everyone up for the next match – always the crucial game in football.

The only thing you don't do is play. But once you know you can't play anyway, managing is, as I said, the next best thing. All the ex-players I know find that this is so. Some are driving cabs, others are incredibly successful businessmen, but among those who aren't managers I've yet to meet one who doesn't wish he was a manager – that is, still in the game.

I have managed all over the world and I've won a few, lost a few and drawn a few, of course, but whatever the result, whether it worked out or not, all my teams have treated the ball in a special way. I consider it a sacrilege not to go out and play when you can go out and play.

I think there are two schools of management. There is the dictatorial manager and there is the friendly father figure, the counsellor. I'm more the latter, of course. I would never say 'we are going to play 4-4-2 because I say so'. Some managers are like that. They put their drawing up on the board and say this is how we're going to play, and that's it. Take the case of Juan Román Riquelme at Barcelona, for example. He went to Spain from Boca, and Barcelona's Dutch manager Louis van Gaal was after a very interesting type of football, but with a very rigid scheme. Riquelme didn't fit in, so he was sacrificed. He may have been the most expensive player but he was sacrificed.

I've never been like that. I'm more about looking at the players I have and then devising a system that will allow each and every one of them to shine. If I have three very good central defenders I'll try to find a formation that fits all three in comfortably. If I have two very good forwards I'll play them both. If I only have one I'll play with just one. If I have good wingers I'll play them. I like to mould myself to the situation.

And after that you can start to change a bit. Change is very important, as I've said. You must be flexible. You have to permanently adapt to new situations. That is how it is as a player, and it's the same as a manager. If there is a formula that works very well at one club and you go to another club and try to implement the same formula, it won't work. I can of course say this from experience, having moved from Swindon to Newcastle.

You have to adapt to new circumstances. Newcastle is a huge club, the expectations are huge, the players are different.

Each group of players, each club, is a new situation, and within that group/club things are constantly on the move. I always hear that a week is a long time in politics. Well, it's a long time in football too.

The main task of a manager is to remove unnecessary pressures and anxieties from the players. You can never remove the pressure completely, of course, only as much as possible. I always felt that the more relaxed my players were, the less pressure they felt and the better they played. Of course there is an intrinsic pressure that can never be taken away, but I always tried to have their minds as calm as possible at the key moments – just before going out on the pitch, for example. Absolute concentration, I think, is key – no one coming to say hello, no chairmen visiting, no friends, nothing. Concentration and relaxed minds.

I don't like speculating. I think as a manager I'm a little bit like I was as a player. I was never a speculator. I think football is like a chess match. I play chess to a decent standard. One has to defeat the rival one move at a time. Football is the same: you have to establish a tactical superiority, then that superiority will also establish itself mentally, and slowly, move by move, you end up defeating your opponent. Ideally this is done through beautiful play.

That is because football is part of show-business, and this we should never forget. You know, Lionel Messi, Cristiano Ronaldo, Kaka, all the high-profile players who are making all the money . . . that's all down to the fact that there were artists before them. The precision, the science of the game, that's all good and necessary. But in short, the ones who have made a huge difference, the ones who have made football into what it is today, are the artists. Pelé, Cruyff, Beckenbauer, Best, Charlton, Di Stéfano, and more recently Maradona . . . it was them. It wasn't the hard defenders. With all the respect I have for them, it wasn't them who made the game what it is, it was the artists. And I think football owes them a huge debt of gratitude. They are the ones who made football the beautiful game.

The fans just want their team to win, they don't really care how. But when I watch a match I always want the team that is playing better to win. Always. I have always identified with the beautiful game, and with those who defend it. Of course tactics and science are all part of what you need: you have to eat properly, rest properly, tactically you have to have a clear idea of what you're doing on the pitch. But many of the things that will affect the outcome of a match cannot be planned.

When I started at Swindon the fact that I had won a World Cup with Argentina and an FA Cup with Tottenham made a difference. But if all the respect that exists is to last, in the day-to-day working with the players you have to nourish it. So the psychological aspect – the mental dynamics of the group – is the main thing. Players sense weaknesses and favouritism. They sense everything.

As a manager I have always had a very close relationship with my players, but I think if I had to pinpoint one thing I've learned and one thing I intend to work on in the future, it's my treatment of the guys on the bench. This is something I've not been very good at. I'm always told I should address this. I have an excellent relationship with the first-team players but I don't know how to handle myself with the reserves. I think it's because so long as I was fit I was never on the bench myself – well, only a handful of times in my life. As a result I have this enormous difficulty with squad players outside the first eleven. The eleven who will play, I always know who they are and they are special to me. But I think with hindsight I should have respected the others more. Keith Burkinshaw, who joined me as my assistant when I was at West Brom, always pointed this shortcoming out to me. He was always going on about it. A lot of other people close to me, for example,

Steve Perryman, talked to me about this matter too.

I've always been of the opinion that one should go and confront players straight up with the truth. When I have my eleven and they are playing and suddenly one isn't working out and I decide to make a change, it's always tactical. I do it because I think things will go better if A plays instead of B, or B instead of A. That's all. But a lot of the time the player concerned won't accept that. It's the manager's mistake. It's a defence mechanism, because not playing affects your confidence, and if your confidence is diminished you will play less well. It's a fact. In that sense I try to be as honest as possible. Why are you not playing? Because I think we will perform better with someone else on the pitch. That's it. Simple.

Football is very immediate. You don't have many chances to try something out and see if it works. It is the next match that matters, nothing else. It's not the match that has been, it's not the match that comes after the next one, the only match that matters is the next one. And you always have to be ready for whatever may need addressing before, during and after your next match. Nothing else matters. Whatever you're planning or wishing to do, you have to be able to respond if a change in circumstance requires it.

And changes in circumstance happen, whether you

want them to or not. You have Diego in your side. He gets injured. You have to adapt. Say what you like, but you'll have to play another man and almost certainly change your system. Argentina beat West Germany 3–2 in the 1986 World Cup Final, but would they have won without their captain Maradona on the pitch? I think not. I think Maradona was crucial for that victory. It was a relatively poor team elevated to winner status by Diego's presence. Argentina in South Africa in 2010 – will they win it again? Well, if they're all there, Messi, Sergio Agüero and everyone, there's a good chance. But if one of them gets injured, who knows?

Look at Ronaldo just before the 1998 World Cup Final. Brazil reached that final with relative ease. The day of the final, everything fell on Ronaldo – his illness, whatever – and the effect on the Brazilian squad in the camp was destructive. Possibly if the manager had to decide today he would send Ronaldo off to get better and keep all the other players focused and concentrated. But the distraction caused by Ronaldo made them go out and lose in the worst way. France's first two goals were corners. To let any goal in from a corner is bad for a manager, and the only explanation is a lack of concentration. How the best players in the world can lose concentration in a World Cup Final is beyond explanation. They practically handed the trophy to the hosts. And with all the amazing talent that was in that team. And why? Because they were all distracted by their star striker.

As a manager you simply try to cover as scientifically as possible everything you need to take into account – the technical, the tactical, the psychological. But ultimately you're in the hands of God. You can talk for hours and hours about tactics, technique and strategy, but in the end, like everything else in life, luck or chance – the unforeseeable element – also plays its part.

26

Tenets of Coaching

I like to place a lot of emphasis on the technical aspects of football because if I can improve each player by just 10 per cent then the team will improve exponentially. And the players love it when they can see they are doing things better. For example, you take a player and say, 'How well do you shoot with your right foot and your left foot, on a scale of one to ten?' He might answer, 'Well, I'm right-footed and I'd say about eight points for my right and five for my left.' Then you say, 'OK, if you're eight with your right we'll try to get you to nine. Five with your left? Let's get to seven.' And so on.

The purely physical side is also very important. At Swindon, for example, I wanted every single one of my players to be as fit as Real Madrid players. I told them there was no reason why each and every one of them could not be in tip-top condition. We looked at weight (usually players have to lose a couple of kilos), endurance, everything. So the physical fitness and the training is the easiest. That's the science. Obviously you can't turn someone who doesn't sprint into a sprinter, but everyone can always improve.

When I started at Swindon, the manager was much more than a head coach; he was in charge of every aspect of football at the club. It was the same at Newcastle. Now they're more separate, but back then the manager did everything. At Tottenham I would finish training in Mill Hill and drive to the club with my 'kitchen' (the club's core people – a kitchen cabinet, if you like), and there it was like another job. Answering letters, finding out which games were on, checking who was going to which match, dealing with the press . . . It was a big job. Nowadays the admin has been separated a bit from the management so managers are more like head coaches, but the ones who are the most successful are still involved in contracts and so on. They will not deal with the contracts directly, of course, but they will have a very big say in who is bought and sold. The unsuccessful managers tend to be the ones who have teams bought for them. I think this is a little bit like what happened at Newcastle with Kevin Keegan in his last spell at the club. Obviously, clearly, the manager has to choose his squad.

So we have the physical side on the one hand – the easiest – and then the technical side: trying to improve the specifics every day. When I was managing Jürgen Klinsmann, for example, I gave him a high level of training exercises. I shot balls at him and he had to control them, from wherever, at whatever speed. I basically shot at him – *pum!* – and he killed the ball – *tack!* And he learned to control it better. *Pum! Tack!* Touch is so important. The *gambetas* can come later. In the end you have to work on the player little by little: like this . . . not so high . . . yes, like that. It's all about technique.

Then there is the tactical aspect of the game. How will the team form up when it's defending? That's something all managers focus on. They work a lot on defence. I look at defending and attacking in the same way, but attack is harder to plan. You need artists, and if you don't have artists you need imagination. Any manager today can plant a system into the team – this is how we're going to play – but then there are all sorts of subtleties. If one goes forward another must come back, to protect against the counter-attack. It's not that simple. And as I said, the most complicated question of all is this: how do you effectively attack a team that's well organized and waiting for you?

And after all that comes the incredibly important

part of the game that I spoke about in the previous chapter, the psychological factors. There has always existed this controversy in football – psychologists, yes or no? I think the answer is most definitely yes. But the problem is that football has never accepted that. Football culture is wary of psychologists because they're not football people by definition, and football people are very reluctant to accept outsiders. I am open-minded but I wasn't able to bring in psychologists because the ambience in a club, the players, everyone, was against it. And at a big club they are also reluctant because they have big names, and with a psychologist the players will have to open up and tell them things that they can never be sure won't come out eventually, even if it's years later. Yes, I think fear lies at the heart of why psychology hasn't caught on in football. Which explains why a good manager also has to be an extra-ordinary psychologist – Sir Alex Ferguson, for example. And I only mention him because he's the most successful.

A good manager has to be the inspiration for the team. Diego Maradona with the current Argentina squad, for example: he's not going to tell them how to attack or defend because they know that; he has to be the inspiration for the team, the motivator. And never forget you have eleven or more men to deal with, and they're all different. There are some players who, if you take the wrong approach or say something too strongly, will burst into tears and that's that, you've lost them for forty-five minutes, maybe even a month. So you have to find another way.

Generally speaking, I think it's a great advantage as a manager if you're able to do a lot of the things you are preaching. My last minute as a player was in that Swindon match in August 1989 – over twenty years ago now! However, as a manager I continued to train with the players and I was able to show them what I meant, to physically do with the ball what I wanted them to do, or show the exact pressure I was after. I noticed that was a huge advantage.

At the same time what was also very important was that the players saw me as a star, that they recognized me as a big name in football. That always helps a manager to start with. How did Franz Beckenbauer go straight into managing the German national side? Because of who he had been as a player. Take Daniel Passarella at River: he also went straight from playing to managing on the strength of who he had been as a player. Johan Cruyff went directly to Barcelona – same thing. It's a big help, because the players will be thinking, 'He's been a great player, he probably knows a thing or two about this' – even if that's only at the beginning.

There are other theories on how best to start managing, of course. Arsène Wenger, for example, believes one should start with a small team and work one's way up slowly. This point of view is just as valid. It doesn't matter how good a player you were, eventually you have to succeed in turning that into something the players who will go out on the pitch for you can use. But there is a certain kind of respect which at the beginning is a very particular asset. That respect, however, has to be sustained on a daily basis, and not everyone can do it. Pelé tried to be a manager. Bobby Charlton tried, too. Both truly great players, but they couldn't do it. I think both would have loved to manage more but, in short, they never could.

Formally, I trained as a manager when I was still playing at Tottenham, and all big clubs operate like this: players are given the opportunity to do the manager's course without having to go anywhere. They came over from the PFA to train us. There used to be a smaller auxiliary pitch at White Hart Lane – it's not there any more – and on Monday nights we did the manager's course on it. Most players have done it here in England, and for most Premiership players it's a fairly straightforward formality. Because here in England, and I think this is the right attitude, they consider they can't ask someone like me, or any other top-division player, to prove himself in terms of technique, for instance. Even the technically worst player in the Premier League will, in comparison to the ordinary people taking the course, have a vastly superior technique. Loads of people take the course who are not footballers at all, or who play in lower leagues, and they are expected to develop their technical skills and knowledge. But for us top-division players it was more or less a formality, which means that most professional players will also be qualified managers after a certain point in their careers.

I did have to attend an intensive course, for about ten days, somewhere near Birmingham, for the second level. And then, just before the third level, the FA's Charles Hughes stipulated I couldn't do the nationals course, with my fellow players from the Football League, because I was foreign. He turned it into something much more complicated than it needed to be. He wanted me to attend as a foreigner with people from all over the world I'd never met in my life, even though after playing here for over five years I was entitled to do the course as a national. As it turned out I was one of the very first foreign managers in English football.

The English are very practical. They are not prone to fussing over qualifications if your name fits the bill. The chairman doesn't ask for a diploma if he wants a particular person who is available, not to mention a world champion. They are very respectful here of that little medal – it's special. The other day on the golf course, for some reason medals came up as a topic and someone said they had two medals from a war, someone else had another medal, and I had a World Cup medal. Bingo – that's the one that makes people stand up and take notice.

Once there was some big fuss over Johan Cruyff because he refused to do the formal course to get the manager's diploma. 'I'm not doing it,' he said. And of course he went on to manage Barcelona. That issue always crops up. In Diego's case, too: some people say he shouldn't manage because he is not formally qualified as a manager. The formality is not indispensable. If a club wants you they want you, and they have their reasons.

Now they have got stricter with the regulations, I think; there are more barriers. You need not just a licence from the country, you also need a UEFA licence if you're managing in European competitions. In Paraguay I needed a South American licence, an Argentinian one – although actually I think I used my English one. I've certainly never had a problem.

Now that I think about it, I have managed in the Premier League, in the Champions League with Croatia Zagreb, in the Copa Libertadores in South America with Racing, and in the J-League in Japan. When you think about Argentinian managers who have managed in Europe, there are probably only a handful of us who have done it. Basile, Menotti, Bilardo, Bianchi, Passarella, Cúper, Valdano . . . I may be forgetting one, of course. And those who have managed in both the Libertadores and the Champions League? I don't think Basile got to the Champions League, nor did Bianchi, and Valdano never managed in the Libertadores – he never managed in South America. I may be the only one.

27

Ups and Downs at Swindon

To return to my first season as a manager proper, with Swindon in 1989–90, we did really well. We got promoted to the First Division, and we earned that promotion in the best possible way: through playing at Wembley and playing beautiful football.

During that campaign we'd competed against some really big clubs, the likes of Newcastle, Leeds and Sheffield United. The latter two got promoted directly. The fourth-placed team, us, then played the fifth, Blackburn Rovers, in the play-offs, and the sixth (Sunderland) met the third (Newcastle). We beat Blackburn over two legs and at the end of May we played the final against Sunderland at Wembley. Alan McLoughlin scored the goal, and we were up – the first time, I believe, Swindon had ever got to the top division (still called the First Division in those days). The fans celebrated with ticker-tape, just like in Argentina in 1978. I recall it happening at Tottenham once as well. It was wonderful, spectacular.

I went off to Argentina at the end of the season, like I'd done every year since I first arrived in 1978. Except this stay turned out to be quite an interesting one. There was an ongoing financial investigation into Swindon by the Inland Revenue at the time. Indeed, about four matches before the play-off final the taxman had raided the club's offices: it was all over the news. We were in Cornwall at the time. It was about five o'clock in the morning, I was completely fast asleep, and there was a *knock, knock* on my door. I thought it was one of the players messing about and said 'go away', but they insisted and then said 'Police!'

What? Police?

I opened the door and they said they were letting me know, as a courtesy, that our captain, Colin Calderwood, who I would later sign for Spurs, was going to jail – and I mean straight to jail – and all the other players had to return to Swindon immediately where they must supply statements.

Basically, the investigation was about money that was being paid as cash, undeclared. Little extras were being paid out in little envelopes. It was a huge mess, and we immediately contacted Gordon Taylor at the PFA who helped us come to an agreement with the taxman – who wasn't at all interested in the players, for whom we arranged immunity. The deal was that everyone declared, gave their statements, because there had been a sort of pact of silence prior to that.

I was involved a bit by default. I didn't pay the players or anything, but at one point the club secretary blew the lid on it because the chairman, Brian Hillier, sacked him, and on one occasion, maybe when he'd just been sacked, I was asked to give out the envelopes. It wasn't very much money – £150 or so – and I gave it to Colin. That was the only inkling I had about it.

It was fairly common practice, to be honest. I think they wanted to make an example of Swindon, because it wasn't just Swindon that operated like this. I'd be very surprised if it happened in big clubs like Arsenal and Manchester United, but in smaller clubs it was pretty much the norm.

Colin Calderwood had been detained because he was thought to have been distributing the envelopes, and we had to get him released. He wasn't arrested, but he was being 'held', and again Gordon helped us. He was brilliant. 'You're not touching the players!' he said, and we got Colin out, picked him up, and went on to play the final and win promotion to the First Division.

So, back to my summer stay in Argentina, where I

was basking in promotion glory. I received a call telling me that the FA had decided to send Swindon down to the Third Division. This was quite separate from the Inland Revenue's investigation, which went to trial and after which Hillier ended up in prison. The FA had decided to act, and they relegated us.

We decided to fight the FA's ruling. Hillier left and the vice-chairman stepped up. We got an injunction in the High Court. The days passed and the season was about to start but we couldn't start because technically speaking we were in the Third Division even though we were meant to be in the First. And neither could anybody else's season start. The First Division matches couldn't start because we had a fixture we weren't being allowed to play and the Third Division couldn't kick off because of the injunction, the High Court ruling. In the end a common-sense compromise was reached: we wouldn't be relegated but we weren't allowed to go up either. We remained in the Second Division.

It didn't occur to me to walk away. I could have, I suppose. But I was very involved with the club and I felt a sense of loyalty. They'd given me my first chance as a manager, after all. And if I'd left immediately the blow for Swindon might have been too much. I don't know if they would have appealed against the FA's decision, for instance. I liked my squad, they were good players. We probably played the most beautiful football in our division. We didn't have as big a squad as Newcastle, for example, so our achievement was huge.

But the High Court action cost a lot of money so we had to sell some players. McLoughlin was one. Several others had played so well in 1989–90 they took the chance to go to First Division clubs. It was a big blow. You think you've won promotion and then you have to stay where you are, you lose good players, and there's no money to replace them adequately. Colin Calderwood got injured too. We did buy some players – Nestor Lorenzo was the main one – but the team was full of resentment for the way it had been treated and we were soon languishing in mid-table. This was the first hiccup in my managerial career, although through no fault of my own. I would have loved to have seen how that Swindon team would have fared in the big time – the First Division – under my leadership. I've never been relegated as a player or manager and I'm sure that Swindon team could have comfortably stayed in the top division had it been allowed the chance.

In the midst of this crisis Newcastle sacked Jim Smith. It was the end of March 1991, we had just beaten Newcastle in the league, and their chairman directly approached me.

I accepted his offer.

28

The Chosen One

Chris Waddle was a very important player for us at Tottenham, and a great friend of mine. In 1991 he was playing brilliant football for Marseille (the club reached the European Cup Final that year), but happened to be back home in Newcastle on holiday when the club asked him to contact me, and he called me directly one afternoon and arranged a meeting in a hotel near Heathrow. The next day I was Newcastle manager.

It is very rare that the press don't get wind of these appointments before they happen. Usually three or four people are being considered for the job, the press speculate and it's important to be very careful what you say, but in this case it was done very swiftly. I think Lothar Matthäus was also considered, but there were no rumours, no articles or columns on the subject, nothing.

Newcastle at the time was all about Sir John Hall. He wasn't the chairman, he wasn't even on the board, but he was the majority shareholder, and he decided the level of money that was available. Jim Smith, whose job it had been to get the club into the First Division, was a very experienced manager, and when he arrived at St James's Park his view was that in order to win promotion we needed to bring in a lot of players who would deliver instant results. He couldn't wait. So he brought in a lot of players with experience who were at the end of their careers.

When I joined it was looking difficult to get promotion that season. We didn't, in fact. But the following season, 1991–92, I thought, 'Time to start afresh.' I set aside a lot of the older players. I'm often accused of favouring younger players, of seeking only young players, but it's simply not the case. I'm not interested in the age of players, their skin colour, their nationality, their sexual orientation, I'm only interested in whether or not I like the way they play football. And what I noticed at Newcastle was that the older players were struggling. They were finding it difficult, very difficult. So it was out with the lot of them.

I wanted to buy players, and as I said, the person who in short decided whether or not to go ahead with that was Sir John Hall. He said no. I imagine he had to guarantee the funding, or put the money up himself, but I don't know for sure. Anyway, he said no, there was no big pot of money to buy players.

So I looked at the club's youth instead and promoted a load of kids. Some went on to play for England: Steve Howey, for instance, Lee Clark as well, and Steve Watson. Even so, we were obviously going to find promotion difficult. We definitely needed a couple of players with more experience. I tried to mix it up, but in all honesty I just didn't like the older players at the club, I could see they couldn't do it. I could see that, with that squad, we weren't going to make it.

I spoke to them one by one. Some of them didn't take it so well, but a few went on to manage with some success: Roy Aitken, for example, who was assistant manager to Alex McLeish with Scotland and is now at Birmingham; and Mark McGhee. Jimmy Smith had brought in names.

When I got to Newcastle all the players were white. I brought the first black player to the club, Franz Carr, from Nottingham Forest. He wasn't very expensive and I liked his game a great deal. To start with there were some voices saying, 'How can you bring a black player to this club?' But he was good.

We formed a squad that played well but lacked experience, and it was a fairly complicated season. And then there was something of a *coup d'état* in the club and Sir John Hall became chairman. He immediately replaced me with Kevin Keegan.

Of course Kevin was a Newcastle legend, and I think he benefited from the gang of kids I brought up from the youth side. They were very good and eager to learn, and although they needed more time before they were ready for the First Division, that first year with me I think they learned a lot. If you ask them now, many of them have good memories of me. Kevin continued to improve them and also brought in some major stars. He got the squad that was needed and enjoyed un-precedented success.

Two months before I left Newcastle a match had been staged to mark the 100th anniversary of the club. It was part of a big event to commemorate the centenary, with lots of ex-stars of the club invited. Kevin Keegan was one of them. He was in Spain at the time, but he came over for this match and he had been quoted in the press saying he wasn't interested in managing, he wasn't pur-suing a management career, and so on. I don't know that this is so, but I think it was that day, when he came to the centenary match and experienced the warmth of the crowds and the atmosphere at the club, that he was smitten. The football mosquito bit!

In Newcastle I had a beautiful house and I loved my

time there. The club's treatment of me was amazing. Being the manager of Newcastle United is like being the Chosen One in that city. It is a great city that respects football, loves football, lives for football. The stadium was absolutely spectacular, right in the middle of town. And the crowd . . . the fans . . . I noticed that northern friendliness immediately – quite a contrast to southern England. Well, they say Newcastle fans are the best in the world, and they don't say it for nothing. It was a fantastic experience, I have very fond memories of the club and the supporters, and I was sad to leave.

Not broken, though, because football's ways are thus. I returned home to London confident that the phone would ring soon.

29

Promotion and Temptation

In May 1992 I was due to play golf with Bobby Charlton, who had organized a charity tournament with many celebrities involved. With just two days to go I heard from West Bromwich Albion that they were interested in hiring me as manager. I remember phoning Bobby to say I wouldn't be able to play in the tournament and not giving him the details, just saying, 'You'll hear through the press soon enough.' I have a sense, I think, for when offers are serious, when they come for me with intent. And in West Brom's case they came to me very firmly. Still, one doesn't want to call it a done deal too early. Bobby, always the gentleman, wished me the best of luck.

West Brom were in the Third Division at the time, although this was 1992 so for the new season it was due to be renamed the Second Division. It was a bit confusing. Their departing manager, Bobby Gould, had missed out on the promotion play-offs by a sliver – he almost made it but didn't. So he and the club parted company and I was offered the job. Silvia and I drove over, she went for a wander round town, and by the end of the meeting we'd agreed terms. (I remember I got fined for speeding that day!)

As a manager, if I'm offered something I'll almost certainly say yes. It's very difficult for me to say no. A lot of people wait and wait for their ideal job; I'm more about taking whatever offer's on the table. There may be a job here and there I've turned down, but on the whole I've taken all the opportunities that have come my way. It was exactly the same with Tottenham, actually. I could have speculated at the time that some offer might come from Spain . . . But no, if a good proposal is on the table I have to say yes.

My year with West Brom was a fantastic one. It's a great club with a great tradition. I was really happy there. I appointed Keith Burkinshaw as my assistant, and Danny Thomas, who had played with me at Tottenham, joined the staff too. He'd had a very bad injury and had retrained as a physiotherapist. We had a good season and qualified for the play-offs, and then there was a great party at Wembley when we beat Port Vale to secure promotion, and then there was the bus ride back to another superb party, with the mayor of the city and many other people. All the images I have in my head from West Brom are positive; friendly surroundings punctuated by beautiful football.

Meanwhile, back at White Hart Lane, Alan Sugar had stepped up as Tottenham chairman; he'd bought the club in 1991. But there was this issue that Terry Venables was fighting for; he was claiming his hands were tied in terms of resources. He was the chief executive by then, no longer the manager, but was very involved with the football side of things. The established notion was – and I don't particularly share this view – that everyone thought Terry was like the Messiah, in tactical terms, in football terms. The pair of them were the perfect ticket: Sugar's economic power base with Venables' football knowledge.

I'd followed everything that had been going on at Tottenham. It's always been my second home and it hadn't been so long since I was there. I still knew all the players and was very up to date with everything that was happening at the club. And by the time we won promotion at West Brom, in the early summer of 1993, the dream ticket of Sugar and Venables had run into trouble. There were stories in the press about how their partnership had dissolved, that there were serious problems.

Something had to happen: either Terry stayed and

someone else would buy Sugar out, or vice versa, Sugar could stay and sack Terry. Which in the end is what happened. It was surprising in a way, as if no one really expected it even though it was on the cards. It had been coming, but it was still a shock when it happened.

Now I must confess to one of the biggest regrets in my professional life. I think I didn't behave right with West Brom. I didn't do right by them.

I didn't do right by them because I had assured the chairman I would stay at West Brom. Obviously I had won promotion and they wanted me to stay – any manager who wins promotion is wanted – but I also wanted to stay. I liked it there. I was loved by the fans and the feeling was mutual. Publicly and privately I stated my commitment to the club. I believed it at the time. But then Tottenham started making strong moves towards me. And deep inside, Tottenham was my dream.

I went to Argentina for a holiday again at the end of the season, the same as every year, and that was another stay cut short. My great friend and former team-mate John Lacy called me and said the vice-chairman at Spurs, Tony Berry, wanted to talk to me. Then over the phone he asked me if I wanted the job. And I said yes.

30

Putting Out the Fires

Once I knew I'd be managing Tottenham for the 1993–94 season my holiday in Argentina was over. It was obvious I needed to go back to England.

I flew back and went to Alan Sugar's house in Chigwell, Essex. It was a modest little place. I'm joking – it was quite spectacular! He was there with Tony Berry and Douglas Alexiou, another director. I had never met Sugar but Tony and Douglas I knew. Their presence made it a lot less intense, or awkward, for me to deal with Sugar, who could be quite intimidating. The meeting was basically to confirm if I would become the manager or not. I obviously wanted the job, and by the end of the meeting I was the manager.

During the interview Alan Sugar asked me a lot of things, in a very businesslike way. Difficult questions, not flippant little questions, but nothing about money.

We spoke about football: what my philosophy was, what my ideas were. But he always wanted a little more. He didn't let me get away with easy answers. He continually probed.

I always had a very good relationship with Sugar. I'll go further: I liked him. I still like him. He has a reputation as a bully following *The Apprentice* – it's a requirement of the programme. I don't believe he is a bully. I think Alan's demeanour hides an underlying shyness. This is why, I think, he doesn't get involved in niceties or chit-chat – he goes straight to the point. A bit like me, in a way. We had dinner with him several times over the years. We met him in Spain, too, even went to his son's wedding. We often got together with our wives and talked about all sorts of things, not just football. When he had first come to Tottenham with Terry Venables he wasn't a football man but he was a fast learner. He was always asking questions, always interested, always wanting a little more than you gave him. He was never one to stay satisfied with a first response. If he asked, 'Why did we lose today?', for example, and the answer came back, 'Well, we lost because so-and-so didn't take the corner kicks properly', he would always take that as a cue to probe deeper.

I got my first taste of this form of interrogation at

that first meeting. It wasn't so much the questions he asked, more, I think, that he was judging me by my responses to them.

It was a very complicated time at Tottenham. The rupture of the 'dream ticket' had produced two sides, both strong and each markedly opposed to the other. The animosity was so intense that it ended up in a well-publicized lawsuit at the High Court (that was later, though). There was a split among the press, too, the *Sun* on the one hand and the *Daily Mirror* on the other, listening to one side and then to the other. And the club was practically completely divided, some players even going to Sugar's house demanding Terry's return.

So when I became manager it was like being in charge of a team in a cauldron. We were putting out fires all over the place. Spurs is by far the club where I had the most troubles. I think when a club catches fire in this way the question is always, 'Who can put it out?' And the reality at Tottenham in 1993 was that there were two people who could have a decent go. One was Glenn Hoddle and the other was me.

To backtrack a little bit, when I left Swindon I left on very good terms. I was asked who could come along to replace me and I suggested Glenn. I thought he would be a very good manager. He did go to Swindon and in fact in 1993 the club got promoted to the Premier League under Glenn.

I remember the end of that 1992–93 season so well: on the Saturday West Brom got promoted to the First Division and on the Sunday Glenn's Swindon got promoted to the Premier League. So we were both enjoying really positive repercussions in that summer of 1993, spectacular publicity. It was Glenn's first job, and even though I had a little more experience, he had made it from the second to the first tier whereas I had gone from the third to second. In short, I think Tottenham went after Glenn first. But he also had an offer from Chelsea. He'd been playing in Monaco but he had left behind a very good reputation – he left behind this good image everywhere he played, of course. Glenn chose Chelsea. It's my own opinion and it's no more than an informed guess, but I think he felt Chelsea didn't have as many problems. I think he judged the situation at Tottenham and got the right measure of it. But I wouldn't want to put words into his mouth. I don't actually know why he turned down Spurs and took on Chelsea. Maybe he knew, deep inside, that he would one day return to White Hart Lane.

When Glenn made himself unavailable, I got offered the job. Many of the players at the club at that time were players I had played with; a lot of them, in many ways,

I had helped teach how to play: they had come up to the first team in their late teens and I was already a veteran, so to speak. I often hung out with them and got on with them really well, and undoubtedly with several of them I had a very good relationship. Yet the situation was tense beyond anything imaginable. One of the players, Neil Ruddock, club captain at the time and a key player for us, decided to leave. And I had been to his wedding. When I spent that season playing in the US, Neil had come with his wife to Florida and they spent their honeymoon with us. But Neil said, 'I'm leaving,' and he left. He had an opportunity to go and play for Liverpool, and in short he forced a departure, perhaps leaving in not the best possible way.

In fact all the stars at the club wanted to leave. It was as if Tottenham was a red-hot iron that had to be dropped quickly. The only ones who didn't say anything were the ones who couldn't find something better than Tottenham. The ones who had options were all very keen to leave.

I knew the situation at the club was chaotic, but I hadn't reckoned on how hard it would be for me to overcome all this. As I said, a lot of the players I knew well and had played with, but some of the new players had been brought in by Terry Venables. They responded to Terry and were clearly 'his' players, and that was

July 1978. Ricky and I got a great welcome from the Spurs fans.

Liam Brady of Arsenal was one of my great opponents and later played in my testimonial.

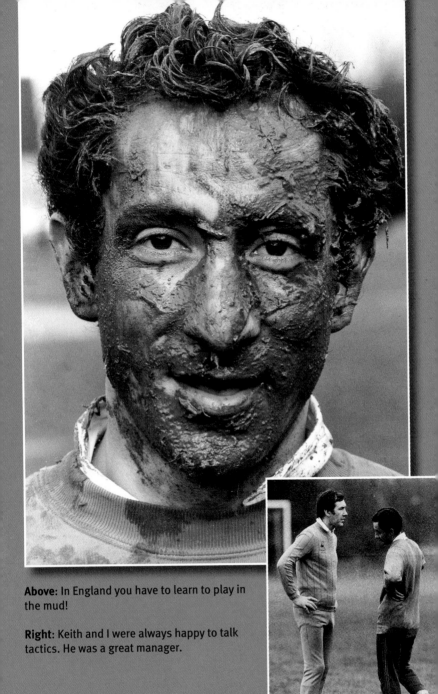

Above: In England you have to learn to play in the mud!

Right: Keith and I were always happy to talk tactics. He was a great manager.

Above left: Ossie's Dream: The 1981 FA Cup.

Above right: After the match with (*left* to *right*) Steve Perryman, Peter Shreeves, Steve Archibald, Paul Miller and Micky Hazard.

Right and below: With Ricky the morning after – what a great midfield! – and (*below*) with Glenn Hoddle.

Above: Diego. At the 1982 World Cup, which proved such a disappointment, and with his wife Claudia.

Below: Maradona played for Spurs! This was my testimonial in May 1986, with my boys Pablo (*left*) and Fede (*right*).

Above left: Paris was beautiful but it was an unhappy time for me.

Above right: Don't mess with Ossie!

Right: Spurs won the UEFA Cup in 1984 but I didn't feel I deserved my medal.

Below: Tackling Liverpool's Paul Walsh towards the end of my Spurs career.

Left and below: Moving into management with Swindon. With the chairman Brian Hillier *(left)* and celebrating our playoff victory in 1990 *(below)*. For some reason I am hiding my glass!

Left: Ecstasy at Wembley again as West Brom gain promotion in 1993.

Left: Managing Tottenham was another dream come true. No longer an apprentice, with Alan Sugar!

Right: With Ilie Dumitrescu and Jürgen Klinsmann (*right*).

Left and below: With my assistant Steve Perryman, who stood by me through good times and bad.

Above: Football has taken me round the world and I had a great time and success in Japan. With the Shimizu S-Pulse fans (*left*) and in costume before the Tokai Cup (*right*).

Below: Celebrating winning the J-League with Yokohama Marinos in 2000.

where I had the most conflicts. I don't remember any at other clubs, but at Tottenham it was difficult. It is a big club so I suppose it's normal for it to be that way. And players at big clubs tend to have big egos.

Essentially, the players were against Sugar. I don't think they were that united among themselves – they couldn't be that united in the midst of so much chaos. Such situations force people to focus on their own survival, I think. But they were united in one respect: they didn't think Alan Sugar was the right person to be at the helm of the club.

I spoke to them quite a bit, individually. A key figure at this time was Teddy Sheringham, the leader of the team. I don't want to say anything against Teddy but he was very much Terry's man. He had been brought to the club by Terry, he had been top scorer the year before, and he was very loyal to Terry, and outspoken about the fact that he didn't agree with Sugar sacking Venables. Teddy was an excellent player and always a consummate professional, able to perform his functions. He and I actually had a very good relationship. But the resentment lay under the surface; it was in the dressing room, it was in the atmosphere.

He then had his own confrontation with Alan Sugar, because he had requested a rise in his contract for having been top scorer the season before and Sugar had refused. Generally I try to stay out of such disputes. I try to stay out of the money side of things. If someone else can do it, so much the better. I'm not comfortable with money; I prefer to focus on tactics and football. But in Teddy's case of course I got involved. I was very much in the middle because they had a very bad relationship, Teddy and Sugar.

Then Alan Sugar brought in Claude Littner as chief executive of the club, and that was when for me the problems got worse. If I have one criticism, one thing to say to Alan Sugar, it would be that I didn't like the fact that this person came along. There were some administrative issues at the club; it was obvious Tottenham had to move on to another level in terms of its management and its finances – the way all big clubs are today, in a sense. But the way things were handled wasn't quite as professional as one would expect in a big club nowadays.

Littner basically started to cut budgets and expenses. There were some aspects of this that needed looking at, but there were a lot of things being axed which simply generated more problems within the squad than any saving could possibly offset. At the time there was a lot of nonsense being talked about the players' cups of tea being cut, which was just that – nonsense. But things like stipulating one masseuse instead of two . . .

nowadays it's acknowledged that you need three or four at least. Or, for another example, questioning why we took nineteen players instead of eighteen to an away game ('well, in case there's an injury, or a stomach bug') . . . nowadays it's acknowledged that big clubs will take up to twenty-four players. The constant request for explanations was very difficult. I don't know if it's true that the chief executive stopped paying for the tea for parents who went to watch their kids in the youth sides, but it's at least an indication of the atmosphere at the time, the kind of thing we were thinking about and discussing. It erodes the mood in the dressing room.

It led a lot of the players to complain directly to me. Eventually it led to a full-blown confrontation between Claude and me. I felt he was undermining my authority. We went to see Alan Sugar at his house and I felt Sugar didn't lean one way or the other; he heard us both but I felt he was sitting on the fence. He really should have said 'this is how it is'.

I'm not a confrontational person at all and I wouldn't knowingly or purposely go looking for conflict, but there were things going on that just couldn't be the way they were. Not with everything else that was happening. It was a time when the club should have been concentrating on keeping the good players it had happy, on trying to win them over, bring them over to Sugar's side, on generating a sense of team and shared purpose. Instead, as I said, I felt I was permanently having to put out fires.

The issue of Teddy's contract remained unresolved, and as if that wasn't enough he then picked up an injury. He was in and out of physio; he had treatment with all sorts of specialists. I had never been to a specialist when I was a player. Anyway, I felt things just had to be resolved and I went to see Claude one day specifically to talk about Teddy's contract – and I realized that instead of working towards finding a way to keep Teddy at the club, the opposite was going on. So I had been doing the impossible trying to retain Teddy. It seemed Claude had been thinking all along that maybe we could find another player on half the wages who was just as good. I think Teddy knew that I was desperate to keep him and keen to fight for him. He was my best player. I wanted him to stay at the club, be well, fit and happy.

Another player involved in a saga was Gary Mabbutt. He was one of my very best friends, since the days when we played together under David Pleat. Gary, famously, has diabetes. He used to live next door to John Lacy, and one night we were playing at White Hart Lane and Gary hadn't turned up. It was really unlike him, so I said to David's number two, Trevor Hartley, 'Gary's not here,' and his answer was quite short, something like, 'You worry about yourself, he knows what he has to do.' But I had a feeling something was up and I rang John's house because John wasn't playing that night. He had in fact already left for the stadium because he was coming to watch the game, but his wife Jane answered and I said, 'Would you mind popping round to Gary's because he hasn't turned up at the ground.' She went round, found him lying on the floor in the middle of a hypoglycaemic attack, and called an ambulance. Gary had a few incidents like this, but this one was a potential disaster. He used to joke that I saved his life.

Gary was the club captain and for me a hugely important ally. He was then involved in a terrible incident with John Fashanu, when John's elbow fractured his skull. It was quite serious. I went to see Gary in hospital. I didn't usually go to hospital to see players, but this was Gary.

It seemed the injury had been intentional. Gary is a very good person and he didn't want to make a fuss but we requested to view the replays of the incident because it was a bad injury, and the more we viewed it the more it looked intentional. Fashanu pulled out the racism card and got all the press going and the saga blew up to the extent that we were summoned by the FA. Eventually it was so clear to me, from every angle, that it had been intentional. But Gary refused to act, playing the good guy. He didn't want any trouble, and in the end nothing happened.

After ten years at Spurs Gary's testimonial was coming up. Jorge Valdano was managing Real Madrid at the time so I contacted him to see if we could stage a game against the Spanish side. This is all by way of explanation of how I would move heaven and earth for Gary. Because . . . well, the relationship between player and player and between manager and player can be quite different. When I returned to White Hart Lane as manager, our relationship underwent a change and we became more distant from each other. Now, I'm happy to say, things have got back on track.

Basically, that first year didn't start off so badly on the pitch. That was the amazing thing. Results were with us. My first match as Tottenham manager – this is the way football goes, you know – was at Newcastle. It was obviously a very special place to go, but I didn't have any hard feelings. In fact I had a good relationship with Kevin Keegan, who had replaced me at St James's Park. We won that game, and then won again at Liverpool. Teddy was scoring lots of goals, we were high up the league.

And then Teddy got injured. At Old Trafford. And he was out for maybe six months. I don't want to exaggerate, but it was about that long. And that, combined with Gary being out and Darren Anderton too, was the turning point. When Teddy returned he made all the difference in the world, because of his talent and his leadership and everything. But we'd gone a long stretch without him and we were close to the relegation zone. The season ended up as a big disappointment.

In the midst of all this a *Panorama* programme went out which was an investigation into Tottenham's affairs. It was *à la* Swindon but involving a lot more money, and a lot more sophistication in every sense. The outcome was that Tottenham was punished for the following season, 1994–95: six points deducted, not allowed to play in the FA Cup, and a hefty fine that ran into the order of millions.

31

Audere est Facere

The hardest thing that's happened to me in my life was leaving Tottenham. The blackest time, after the Malvinas aftermath, was my departure from Tottenham.

My life changed completely after that.

Tottenham is my home, my family, everything. I sincerely believe, have always believed, that I was destined to manage Tottenham. There is a way of being that we share, a footballing identity that both I and the club have. I've always known that if I was asked to manage Barcelona, Real Madrid, any legendary club or Tottenham, I would choose Tottenham every time. Without hesitation. I was born to play for Tottenham and to manage Tottenham.

So when I did get to manage Tottenham it was quite literally a dream come true.

As with all dreams, however, once they become a

reality one has to deal with the reality bit as well. And for me it was a very tough reality. I've never quite got over the hurt of how things turned out. I spent years not going back to the club at all. Not once, for many years. Now I do go to games and feel closer to the place again, but until very recently if you asked me when did I finally get over all the disappointment I would honestly have to say, 'Oh, any day now . . .' I am over it now, and really feel part of the Tottenham family again.

I think it's worth looking in a bit more detail at what went wrong. There were, as always, many factors that affected how things turned out. On the pitch and off it.

The football side of things is always the most important for me, but my memories of that time, especially the first year, are shrouded in problems of the personal and institutional type. It was a chaotic first year and I felt completely worn out by it. Too many problems. Until then I had almost never had a confrontation with anyone in England; now I pretty much fell out with everyone. I didn't want to fight or confront anyone, it was just the circumstances. There seemed to be dissent, discord, discomfort everywhere you went. And the press were obviously doing their job, digging out the stories . . .

One of those stories concerned Ray Clemence, who

had had an exceptional career at Liverpool and, quite surprisingly, came to join us for the 1981–82 season. We played for a long time together and I think Ray was one of the best goalkeepers in Tottenham's history. Him and Pat Jennings, both for Tottenham and internationally for England and Northern Ireland – were great players.

I would like to set the record straight with respect to Ray, because when I was manager of Tottenham a lot of people think I sacked him. I want to take this opportunity to say this is absolutely not true. To put it simply, what happened is that when I arrived my assistant was going to be Steve Perryman. Keith Burkinshaw, who had been my assistant at West Brom, took over as manager there. Steve and I had talked about this a lot – we had a gentlemen's agreement: if either one of us got a job managing a First Division club we would take the other as assistant. Even though years had passed and he was managing Watford, I thought Steve was the ideal person to be my assistant at Tottenham and he accepted and joined me. I thought it obvious he was the man for the job: he had played for the club for nearly twenty years, played more matches than anyone else for Spurs, and he shared my vision of football.

The problem was that Ray Clemence, with Doug Livermore, was still there. They had managed the team the previous season under Terry Venables. But when I brought in Steve as my assistant Ray decided to leave. He could have stayed on as first-team coach, and definitely as goalkeeping coach, but he decided to leave. The press made it sound like I had sacked him, which I definitely didn't do. The press will always look for the conflict angle when it comes to big clubs, try to turn the smallest thing into a big story. When Ray decided to leave I brought in Pat Jennings as goalkeeping coach. I thought this was the dream ticket – me, Steve, Pat and Chris Hughton. It didn't turn out that way, as history tells us.

I do feel it's important to put up my hand and claim my share of responsibility for this, and I would like now to try to discover what went wrong in the context of the football philosophy I so ardently believe in.

Firstly, a brief recap of the school of thought that shaped me. César Menotti, who was, and always will be, my number one teacher, advocated what we call in Argentina *el achique*, which essentially means a consistent pressure on the opponent. Basically, having the ball all the time is the main aim. This is a simplification of César's thinking and it's a simplification of my thinking by extension, but when you have the ball the main aim is not to lose it. Keep it, keep it, and only ever risk it in an important move – to score, or to assist someone who can score. If you lose it, immediately regroup and organize everyone on the field to recover it. In their 2009 Champions League Final against Manchester United, Barcelona gave a masterly display of this type of football, and won the game. The key thing is for the rival to have the ball as little as possible. Nowadays you get possession stats on the screen; back then they weren't shown on TV, but if you were watching the game you could see if things were working.

I also believe strongly in the counter-attack. When your opponents lose the ball they are likely to be disorganized, to have players out of position, and there will be spaces as a result, so the first priority has to be to enable a counter-attack by looking for those spaces.

And Tottenham's mantra is 'if you don't risk you don't win'. That's the club motto: *audere est facere*, to dare is to win. It may sound obvious to some. If you want to get to a superior level it's clear that if you don't risk anything you will not gain anything.

My time at Tottenham as manager has often been caricatured as driven by the 'attack, attack, attack' line. But I never said that. Or 'play, play, play'. It's easy to say that, but the key is *how* will we play? How will we attack? I accept there was probably a certain arrogance on my part – not the decision to field five up front, for example, but maybe in thinking I could make any player play well beyond his capabilities. I have to say, looking back on it now, I can still understand the thinking behind this. And I have always thought all aspects of the game hugely important, defence as well as attack. What goes categorically against my principles is to field a player of lesser quality when a player of higher quality is available. I am still convinced it's possible to play with five up front. The Brazilian dream team had Pelé, Tostão, Jairzinho, Rivelino and Gérson. Not even forwards, they were all number tens!

But my weakness was in defence. I needed a better defence, and it cost me dear.

I know now that a good manager is not the one who adheres to a system regardless and never changes it, rather he who is able to vary according to the players available. In principle I like the idea of four at the back. It feels natural to me. But sometimes you don't have the right players for that and you should have the wisdom to adapt the system rather than ignore the facts.

In all my teams I have found that the main idea should be that the team is balanced. Attack, of course, and constantly ask questions of your opponents. But with balance: if you have no balance, for all the beautiful tricks, possession and delightful play, you let a goal in, and in football the result rules. The lyricism is all well and good, but the first thing is the result. The primary concern must be to win the match, then you can look at everything else. You have more confidence and you can develop your game. And at the beginning of my second season as Tottenham manager, with Klinsmann, with the five forwards, we were winning. But when a team is doing badly, dropping into the relegation zone, a psychological issue develops and you start to believe it's impossible to achieve a victory. All you're aware of are the problems in the team.

All-out attack is something I was never an advocate of, contrary to what many believe, even as a player. I was never one to run up front; on the contrary, I was very conscious of the fact that often I had to sacrifice myself for the team. Especially at Tottenham, I sacrificed a lot of attacking play for the team's sake, in an effort to make the team run smoothly. We used to play with four midfielders – Glenn, Ricky, Tony and me – and of the four the most defensive was me (Tony Galvin was more a winger, of course). For me it was very clear that if I went forward, or if I went too far forward, the holes left behind would be too big. So I was always the person trying to give balance to the team.

And in all my teams I have always sought to play someone who will remain in the midfield – I've always tried to have an Américo Gallego, to put it one way. Sure, I love to give my players freedom, have the left-back running up front, whatever – love it. But I would always rely on that person stood in front of the line of four. He is the insurance. We might at some point lose the ball; he'll be able to slow down the opponent's counter-attack, buying time for our own players to get back.

Yes, the five up front became famous at Tottenham. There was one time before the end came when the results weren't on our side and there I was with Steve Perryman and the rest of the 'kitchen' and I said to Steve – one of the great defensive players, whom I've known almost his whole football life – 'OK, Steve. We're going to tackle these defensive problems with a division of labour. I'll take care of the attacking part and you can look after the defensive issues.' We had twenty-four players. 'I'll take the attackers and you train with the defenders,' I said to him. 'Perfect,' he replied. So I walked off with twenty-one players and left him with three to plan out the defence.

It wasn't really quite like that. But I could see that the team was unbalanced. Looking back, I probably could have sacrificed some of my five forwards, but I didn't like the idea because they were top-class players. It would have meant sacrificing a better player for the sake of fielding a more mediocre one, and I just couldn't get my head round that. It has been done since in English football: Arsène Wenger, for instance, has fielded loads of attacking players. And Manchester United right now – they don't have a defensive midfielder whose role is just that. They all do some marking and defending.

The best team I've seen in my life, Brazil in 1970 with their five forwards, they managed it. Between themselves they created a great defensive unit when defending was required. And look at the Holland team of 1974, another team I've loved all my life. There was Johan Neeskens who was a little bit more defensive, but he was a good playmaker too. The entire team defended amazingly well when it had to, seeking to make life impossible for the opponent. It just meant the ten outfield players had to be a bit more focused.

I think I was hoping to emulate this at Tottenham, but maybe that was our downfall.

32

The End of the Dream

My second season, 1994–95, started with even more problems. We needed to buy players but there wasn't much money around because of the financial issues.

In my first season I had bought a couple of players through the FA's tribunal system. The way this works is that when a player is 'out of contract' there is a time span when one contract has run out and no terms have been agreed for a new one, and at this point one can resort to the FA tribunal to fix a price: if the selling club has not renewed the player's contract the club cannot refuse the sale. And if there is no agreement between the buying and selling clubs then the FA fixes the price. So I brought in two players. Whenever you go through the FA it works out cheaper, because it means whoever owns the player hasn't made much of an effort to retain that player. So the buyer always wins.

Except us, that year.

Colin Calderwood came from Swindon. He had been my captain, I needed a bit of serenity, and I knew him well as an exceptional man. I reckoned we might pay £300,000 for him, offered £500,000, which was rejected, and in the end he cost us over a million. And then we went for Jason Dozzell (again through the FA) from Ipswich. The FA ruled the price to be £1.9 million, which in those days was a great deal of money. With respect, these prices were higher than the players were worth. I thought I was going to buy them relatively cheaply, but this shows how Tottenham was being hit that year. During 1993–94 we'd also bought players like Ronny Rosenthal, a centre-forward from Liverpool, and Kevin Scott from Newcastle. These were players we bought under pressure, to save the day, if you like. They weren't players for Tottenham, I can see that clearly with hindsight. But we had to save the burning potatoes, as we say in Argentina. That whole first year was incredibly wearing and weakening, for all the technical staff but for me especially.

We all sweated Tottenham through every pore, but it wasn't enough. The rift between Alan Sugar and Terry Venables was so profound that it spilled over on to the terraces as well. A lot of the fans were also anti-Sugar and pro-Terry, so there were problems.

Then suddenly, at the start of that second year, an incredible stroke of luck: Sugar signed Jürgen Klinsmann. He'd asked me about it, and when he did so I couldn't believe it. Jürgen was a player on a completely different level, a World Cup star – at the time it was like signing Maradona, more or less. I remember my first thought was, 'I doubt he'll come.' I saw the situation as a difficult one, what with the six points docked and everything. But Sugar spoke with him and he agreed and came over. Then, as I got to know Jürgen – we became very good friends – I understood why he'd come: mainly because he wanted to play in London. Full stop. He's a very special person and it was an immense coup for us.

And then the Romanians joined the squad. Ilie Dumitrescu had just had a very good World Cup. I was asked how I felt when Romania defeated Argentina in the last sixteen, knocking us out. I joked, 'I liked him so much I bought him.' But it wasn't quite like that: we had been watching him for some time. For a long time, in fact. Indeed when he scored twice against Argentina I feared his price tag would rocket. It did go up a bit but we bought him anyway.

Dumitrescu was joined by his colleague Gheorghe Popescu. Jürgen and the two of them were joined by Darren Anderton, who was already capped for England,

and Nicky Barmby, who soon would be. At the back there was Sol Campbell, who was becoming a force to be reckoned with. Our squad was growing in stature. We still had some Achilles heels, of course, but overall I'd go as far as saying that was the best squad Tottenham had had since my time as a player there. Jürgen was easily the best player I've ever managed in my life. And with Teddy recovered from injury, a formidable line-up emerged. Teddy was an exceptional player. With hindsight I can see now that people must have thought with Teddy and Jürgen up front, why would you need any more forwards? But as I've said, for me it's a sacrilege to have an outstanding player and not field him in order to play a mediocre one instead. And I had the two Romanians, Darren and Nicky as well.

This was such a different world to the one Ricky and I had stepped into back in 1978, but there are some universals which never change. The two Romanian players, to some extent, went through similar processes to the ones we'd gone through, and obviously I was able to tell them a lot about my own experiences. I knew exactly what they were going through. There was always the issue of wanting to go home, back to Romania, and as much as I could I would say, 'No problem, go home for a couple of days.' Jürgen never had that problem.

As far as the football was concerned they found it a

little bit harder to adapt. If you look at the Romanian squad of the time, and how football was played in England, it was different. Romanians are more like Latins – they have a different type of game, more of a passing game, more touches. By the mid-nineties England was no longer quite the exact opposite – like when I had first come, when English football was very direct, the ball permanently in the air and the midfield completely bypassed – but it wasn't yet what it is today either. Nowadays all the best teams have everyone coming out playing, which requires a better technique from most men on the pitch. It implies the playing of better football, in fact. As I've said, I think this shift in English football is due in large part to the influx of foreign players, a process that started with Ricky and me and was solidifying by the early to mid-nineties.

Football-wise Jürgen assimilated perfectly and immediately – he had played in France and Italy so he was an experienced international with a proven record in adapting to different clubs and styles. But ultimately he was an outstanding player, and great players can play anywhere.

We started the 1994–95 season by beating Sheffield Wednesday 4–3 away. Klinsmann scored the winner, and then he scored twice in our first game at White Hart Lane, against Everton. The press accused him of diving, all sorts of nonsense, but he became hugely popular and at the end of the campaign was voted Footballer of the Year. He played his first match as if he had always played there. I remember it very clearly, seeing him with Teddy, like they'd been doing it together for years.

I became very good friends with Jürgen. I remember picking him up from the airport when he first arrived – we didn't know then that we would remain close for so many years. I was also the last person he saw before he left England. He left Tottenham long after I did. I offered to drive him to the airport again but he was going on the bus. He's a very special person.

He held his testimonial in Frankfurt, and it was the best testimonial I've been to in my life. Spectacular: private planes, all the trimmings – he even hired Bryan Adams to play a set. He had got together two sides: one was the German national team, with Berti Vogts as manager, and the other team was made up of all the best players from every club he'd ever played for – Monaco, Inter, Tottenham, etc. He could have had any manager for that team, and he chose me. I was very honoured.

I got on very well with Jürgen, but it was a challenge managing him. It was a challenge managing Teddy too. You couldn't get away with saying any old platitude to them; their way of speaking about football was much more sophisticated than that. I always felt I needed to hit the spot with what I wanted to say or suggest. In training, too, you couldn't really get away with giving them basic exercises. You had to find training activities that would be challenging and draw the best from the level those two were at. Because our squad was full of very good players, they could all rise to the challenge.

I relished this aspect of my job. It wasn't all about technique training, though. I have found that the very best players need little coaching in terms of technique but a lot of support in other ways. How you talk to players at such a level . . . you have to really tune in to the psychological side of things. How are they feeling? If they're feeling OK it's all good, but occasionally they need some support because of things going on in their lives, things that affect their mood and by extension the way they play. Jürgen used psychologists more formally when he was in Germany, but he was the exception. We at Tottenham had some contact with the psychologist John Syer who was very good friends with Steve, but not really in an official capacity.

This is a crucial issue. It's very difficult for players to open their hearts or souls to anyone outside the core of their team, 'the kitchen', the hub of the team: the manager, the players who play, sometimes a favoured kitman, sometimes a medic. It's a very closed world. The players know that anything that isn't said there can crop up outside the inner circle. It's a delicate balance to make the players feel like the superstars they are while at the same time protecting them from being superstars and having superstar lifestyles. The amount of press interest in every detail . . . it's so overwhelming when you get to a certain level.

It reminds me of an incident which I can laugh about now but which exemplifies the level of intrusion and exposure. Pat van den Hauwe was going out with a girl who'd been out with one of the Rolling Stones. Or something like that – let's just say she was a very famous girl. Teddy was going out with her sister. It was a tabloid fest. One day we had a run-in, Pat and me, and he was furious with me. I took him off the pitch and substituted him, and he didn't like it. But he told the press that he had tried to throw me off the second-floor balcony of my Tottenham office and that his girlfriend had had to restrain him! Imagine reading that in the paper. So I sent her a bunch of roses, thanking her for saving my life!

Going back to the psychologists and the kitchen, as I was saying, it's very difficult for a player to open up to a psychologist. If that psychologist was part of the 'kitchen', however, it would be different, but I think it's going to be hard for that switch to happen in football.

Managing that Spurs squad was a fantastic experience, and the football was a joy. The group was a strong one, and with international superstars from the World Cup added to the ranks the season ahead was full of promise. But in spite of these positives I felt that my margin for manoeuvre was limited. Off the pitch things were still so chaotic, and another big blow for me was the departure of Vinny Samways.

Vinny had come up from the youth side when I was a player at White Hart Lane. I had got to know him when he was only thirteen: he always came to practise with us. I had taken him under my wing a bit, perhaps because he reminded me a lot of myself as a young player. I think we were similar. By the time he left he was a very important player in the squad. He chose to go to Everton, but I felt we should have been able to retain him. I felt he left because of all the tensions at the club, and as I said, it was a blow for me.

To top it all, Terry Venables, in the midst of his bitter battle with Sugar, was appointed manager of England. My God! Sugar was saying, 'I don't care if he is the manager of England, he's not setting foot in White Hart Lane!' But Venables was the national manager so he needed our players: Teddy, Darren, Nicky, Sol. Once again the players were pulled right into the middle of the conflict. There was permanent tension.

So that second year was both sublime and painful. The irony was, I guess, that shortly after I left the club the FA revoked the six-point deduction, allowed the club to compete in the FA Cup and upped the fine instead. The fine had been the least of my worries; it was all the other stuff that was insurmountable. Oh well. Too late for me.

The season had started well with those wins against Wednesday and Everton, but as it progressed there were a few results that weren't exactly good for us and the whole five forwards issue was aired again. Perhaps I was too stubborn. Who knows? I can see now that if you have Jürgen and Teddy what do you want three more forwards for? Then again, as I've said, look at Brazil in 1970. It can be done. Still, we clearly lacked a couple of players to balance the defence.

The key match, the one I got sacked after, was against Notts County in the Coca-Cola Cup. The night of 26 October 1994 was wet, dark and cold – horrible. When we arrived at Meadow Lane with Tottenham and all its stars I remember feeling that it was a recipe for disaster.

We had already conceded two goals in the first half when Dumitrescu got sent off (he needed something like that to happen in order to understand that certain things can't be done in English football, such as diving, protesting, getting worked up in a Latin way). We were down to ten men. We lost the tie 3–0.

I think of it as my black night. I knew my time was up.

We beat West Ham in the league three days later, so at least I left on a win, but the next day Alan Sugar fired me (although he never actually said 'You're fired'). I genuinely think he was sorry. He had to do it, in a sense. He felt a change was necessary. The fires had been quashed, the squad was superlative, and he thought another manager could pick the baton up and run with it.

In hindsight I should not have gone to Spurs when I did. I should have waited for the opportunity to manage the club later in life. Looking back on it now, I see it this way. As it is, I feel I arrived at Tottenham then left Tottenham, and it's as if that closed a whole chapter for me in England.

33

The Emperor's New Clothes

Yes, leaving Tottenham was a hugely traumatic thing for me. Almost on a par with the Malvinas conflict in 1982. Again, everything was related to Tottenham.

I played a lot of golf. I have always used this game as a means of shutting everything out – the good and the bad. Golf makes you concentrate so much on each shot, each hole, that you forget everything else.

I had the impression that doors in England were shut for me. It's not that I chose to go and manage in every country I eventually went to – far from it. A lot of managers after a bad experience go to a smaller club and start building their career again. Maybe if I had stayed in England that would have been the case with me too. But there was interest in me from abroad and I was eager to keep working so I took a job in Mexico with Chivas.

Mexico is economically the number one country in Latin America. There is more money in football there than there is in Brazil or Argentina. I think only Boca in Argentina and São Paulo in Brazil are on a par with the Mexican clubs in terms of budget. So for an Argentinian or Brazilian player the dream destination is first Europe, second Mexico. The top players of Argentina and Brazil come to Europe, and then there's a second crop of very good players who go to Mexico. The First Division in that country is therefore very competitive.

At that point, for sixteen years all my football culture had been English, as a player and manager. Mexicans say *Mexico es un mundo* – 'Mexico is a world of its own' – which it is, in a way. So many different cultures: the legacy of the Maya and Aztec Empires combined with the influence by European Imperialism and then having the US as neighbours has created an amazing mix. The lifestyle was similar to Argentina. In Guadalajara, where I was, the climate was always favourable, and it reminded me of Córdoba.

The hardest thing was leaving the kids in England. They were at secondary school and it would have been too disruptive to take them. Luckily Juana was here. Still, it was hard. As they grew older it became easier, but that first job abroad I found it difficult to be so far from them.

Chivas is the most popular team in Mexico. One of the main reasons for that is that only Mexican players can play there. It's club policy, like with the Basques at Athletic Bilbao. The manager can be foreign, obviously, hence my being there, but all the players have to be Mexican. This is an advantage on the one hand and a disadvantage on the other. The advantage is that this makes it an incredibly popular club. The only other Mexican club even close in terms of popularity is América. To give you an idea what this means, when we played at home against América they had maybe 10 to 15 per cent of the fans in the stadium. When we played against them away in Mexico City, half the stadium was supporting Chivas. Wherever we went to play we had a lot of support – a bit like Boca in Argentina. As they say in Mexico, 'You'll always find a Chiva brother.'

The disadvantage is that when Chivas wants a player it always has to pay more because everyone knows they're limited to Mexican players only. The price might be a certain sum for most clubs, but for Chivas it's a bit higher. This can get complicated.

When I arrived, though, the transfer window was over and we couldn't buy any players. We had some very good players in the squad, that was clear, but there was also a need for fresh blood in some crucial positions. The first thing we lacked, and I noticed this as soon as I got there, was a centre-forward. We had two or three but only one of them was of a good standard, and he got injured. This meant that we played beautifully but didn't score. After four months the results weren't good enough, and it was goodbye.

My confidence was on the floor after my experiences at Tottenham, and for a manager confidence is even more important than for a player. Now I'd just suffered a second big blow in a row. I had signed a one-year contract, but after only four months I was back on the golf course in north London!

Almost immediately, less than a fortnight later, a job in Japan came up. Shimizu S-Pulse had requested CVs from a number of managers and I got the job. Steve Perryman came with me, and that was good news for me. We signed a one-year contract again. All my contracts in Japan were for a year. If you succeed, you're offered another year.

Japan was an experience, a different world, totally and completely different. It was also a very successful experience: we won the cup that first year, and in my third year there, 1998, I won Manager of the Year. On the other hand I think I missed English football, even Argentinian football – perhaps a more Western style of football. Football in Japan was just starting at that time and I felt I missed the passion, the competitive edge, all the turmoil of the established mainstream leagues.

I had always been in the eye of the storm, but in Japan there was none of that. The J-League, when we got there, was only just starting to get organized professionally. Most of the managers were from all over the world – Argentina, Brazil, Europe. Since then the J-League has established itself to the extent that Japan has participated in the last three World Cups and won the Asian Cup three times. Before then they would turn up at the Asian Cup if they were lucky, lose, and go home. The transformation has been incredible.

We arrived, as I said, during the early stages of this transformation. The clubs were incredibly professional, though. Physically the players were fit, on a par with the top clubs in the world. Technically too, they were in fact quite good – not up to the standard of England or Argentina but close. The hardest thing in Japan was the tactical side, and this is the same in Africa, I think: you see many individually exceptional players but they struggle to find the tactical discipline, which is what enables sides to win matches.

It's something I've stressed already, and it's worth repeating: there is an enormous difference between being a magician with the ball and knowing how to play football. However skilfully you can perform the tricks, if you don't have the intelligence to make decisions on the pitch, decisions that will serve the team as a whole, you don't know how to play football. A technically limited player who knows what to do on the pitch can be more of an asset than a magician who falls short of understanding the game. Reinaldo Merlo comes to mind, though I realize the name might not mean much to Europeans. At River he knew exactly what he had to do on the pitch even though technically he wasn't that gifted.

It's the emerging football nations that struggle with this more intangible understanding, or knowledge, of how to play football. In the case of Japan it was definitely the area they found the hardest; it's the same for any country not soaked in a football culture in the same way the likes of Argentina, Brazil and Spain are. It can be learned, but it takes time and a lot of hard work.

The Japanese players were very willing to learn and they were very respectful of me as a manager. In fact, they used to call me *sensei* – 'teacher'. We also had time to work: the matches there are only weekly, so we could take it slower, work in the morning and in the afternoon; there was a lot more time between matches. It was amazing the improvements we achieved in the first six months. I was a very technical player. If I hadn't had the technique I had I wouldn't have been the player I was. So I recognize the importance of technique. But technique alone is not enough. It has to be implemented in a tactical scheme in which it makes sense.

After a superb three years I felt I had accomplished what I had set out to achieve and decided to leave. Steve was going to stay on as manager so from the point of view of the club I wasn't letting anybody down. It was all good. No trauma.

For my last match the stadium was filled to its thirty-five thousand capacity and the people were clamouring for me not to leave, stretching their arms out and wanting to shake my hand. It was hugely powerful from an emotional point of view. I went round the pitch, almost like a victory lap, to say goodbye . . . all those hands stretching out . . . uff! Those emotions – incredibly strong.

There and then I decided I would never leave a club again. If I got the sack, fine, but I would never leave myself. I still feel bad about the way I left West Brom, for example, it's one of my very few regrets. I don't know how I could have done it differently, because I couldn't really say at the time of signing 'If the Tottenham job comes up I'm off', but all the same, I could have handled it differently. Now here I was again, deciding to leave Shimizu, a club where the fans adored us and recognized what we were doing on the pitch, where our efforts were paid off with results . . . as I said,

I made a conscious decision never to leave a club again.

The only exception I made was years later at Huracán. But that's another story. Altogether I ended up spending seven years in Japan, all of them great, but after those first three years I missed the Football League action I'd got used to. I missed England, and I also wanted to be available should an opportunity come up in Argentina. Many of my former team-mates were managing there by then – Passarella, Gallego, Brindisi, and so on. I used to watch them and think, 'I wouldn't mind that.' Basically those were the two footballing arenas I missed, the two leagues I followed very closely. I craved the idea of being back in the eye of the storm, in England or in Argentina.

I'd learned some important lessons in Japan, management lessons. For example, before I arrived the club had bought an Italian player, Daniele Massaro. He was lauded everywhere for being Italian, for having scored for Milan in the Champions League Final, for being a world champion; he had played in the best leagues for the best clubs. When I got to Shimizu I picked the eleven players I thought would be the best, including Massaro. Almost immediately I realized he was the problem with the side: his pedigree, if you like, intimidated the other players (certainly when he left they were more relaxed), but also I felt he wasn't performing the way I expected him to, or rather the way he ought to have. So I felt it was important to form a team without him. Not that it was an easy decision, of course. I would have loved to keep Massaro in my team. I greatly admired him and his achievements. But the best thing I did was say, with no qualms, '*Afuera*' – 'Away with you'. As I said, the effect on the other players was instant: they acquired the confidence they'd been lacking, and they understood I was not someone prone to favouritism or succumbing to pressure. And this was a player the club had spent a lot of money on, they had stretched financially to buy him. I think I survived because results went with me – they proved me right. But it was a very important thing to do.

At one point I came very close to managing the Japan national squad, very close. I had all the attributes they were looking for and there was a poll among the fans and it turned out I was their favourite. Arsène Wenger was also toying with the job, saying 'no, yes, no, yes'. I think he was maybe using it a little for his negotiations with Arsenal at the time, and eventually of course he chose Arsenal. Someone he had suggested, Philippe Troussier, was appointed for the Japan job in the end.

I think that's still one of my remaining dreams, or attainable ambitions I should say: to manage a national side. I think I am ideally suited to the role, and I think I

would enjoy managing at national level a bit more
than the day-to-day club stuff. So if there is something
of an Ossie football dream pending, that is it. I would
love to take a squad of players to a World Cup. That
would be great!

34

Political Football

I left Japan feeling I had accomplished what I set out to do. I was looking for a new challenge. The option that came up first was in Croatia. At first I wasn't that interested, but I happened to be invited to Croatia for something else and when I saw the place I was tempted. And Dinamo Zagreb was the biggest club in the country. The Balkans War had only recently finished but the football was healthy: Croatia had come third in the 1998 World Cup in France and there were at least three players from that squad at Dinamo Zagreb, including Robert Prosinecki.

I call it Dinamo Zagreb, but actually that year the club changed its name. Everything that had had the word Dinamo, Locomotiv or some other communist reference attached to it, all of that Soviet-era stuff was abolished. So the club was now called Croatia Zagreb. Our fans – we had the biggest fan base in the country – then boycotted us, so we played in a near-empty stadium. And I can tell you, when only three thousand turn up for a game in a stadium with a sixty thousand capacity, it feels very surreal.

Our main objective was to qualify for the 1999–2000 Champions League, and to do that we had to play the champions of the Hungarian league, MTK, over two legs. The winner would go on to the Champions League and the loser to the UEFA Cup – an enormous difference in prestige, income, everything.

We didn't start out that well because our first match was our home leg and our English friend Graham Poll sent off our number ten. So we played ten against eleven, which was a big disadvantage, and the match finished goalless. But when we went to Budapest for the away leg we beat them and made it into the Champions League.

In our domestic tournament we came first, with no defeats. We only had one serious rival, Hajduk Split; all the other clubs were not so strong and we were head and shoulders above them. We had the best players in Croatia, and Croatia had very good players. The market has opened up since then and there are now players from Brazil and other countries in the Croatian league. But our team was strong when I got there. I didn't need reinforcements. In Japan I did buy an Argentinian player, and I think that was one of the underlying factors of my success there – Fernando Oliva was our Player of the Year – but in Croatia I had no need to buy anybody. The squad was very strong and professional. Prosinecki, for example, was one of the very few players who have played for both Real Madrid and Barcelona. He was the best player in Croatia, incredibly talented.

Maybe it was because of him that in the end I left the club – or was made to leave, to put it more accurately.

For the Champions League matches there was no boycott – the stadium was always packed. The violence between the fans was absolutely terrible, hair-raising. The clashes outside the stadium were extreme – even inside the grounds incidents could escalate; I was once hit on the head by a missile while playing Hajduk Split away!

We started off in mid-September with a fixture against Manchester United, at Old Trafford. They were the reigning European club champions and we were very much the guests at their wedding, but we managed to draw 0–0. We flew back to Zagreb and the President's guard of honour was waiting for us. But it then got complicated. We lost to Marseille when we shouldn't have. Then we played Austrian side Sturm Graz and won easily at home, but in the second match against them, which was absolutely key, we lost 1–0.

At that time, towards the end of October, Prosinecki, our number one player, picks up an injury. The second match against Manchester United is due, at home. It's a huge fixture, the stadium will be packed, but there's a big question mark hanging over Prosinecki. He's not fit to play the full ninety minutes and I don't want to start him because I don't want to wear him out unnecessarily. I think I'm going to put him on the bench as this match is going to be very physical. United have Roy Keane, in his prime. Giggsy, Scholes, they're all in their prime. So I speak to him. 'To start with it will be very physical on both sides,' I argue, 'and then you'll come on and make all the difference with your talent.'

'I'm not sitting on the bench,' he replies, which a day before the match is rather a big problem.

Prosinecki spoke Spanish and was one of the few players with whom I could communicate fluently. He was a great guy, generally. He felt fit and he thought it was some sort of dishonour to start on the bench. Much as I had felt as a player. I guess I had inadvertently transmitted this as a manager to my players. But in certain cases I had been able to accept being on the bench – the 1984 UEFA Cup Final was one. Start on the bench, and if you're necessary for your team you play, if not, why risk worsening an injury or playing below par?

I came under a lot of pressure to start him. A lot of pressure, from the press, the chairman, everyone. But I was adamant. I wanted to do what I thought was best.

Eventually, after a saga that included him threatening to leave the training camp, he started on the bench, came on and made a fantastic play which led to our goal. But we lost 2–1, which complicated everything for us.

And that day the fans were heated, very tense. The president of the club was the mayor of Zagreb, a political character by definition. All the terrace chants were 'Dinamo, Dinamo!' even though by law the club had had to change its name. There was a lot of animosity surrounding that issue. During the matches against Manchester United the fans clamoured for the president's resignation. It had become a highly charged situation.

The following day the club president called me in. We were doing really well, we were top of the domestic league, and even though this last match had made it harder we were still in with a chance, with one match to go, of making it to the next stage of the Champions League. But I think in a way the president felt he might dispel the tension among the fans if he changed manager. And that's how my adventure in Croatia ended.

It was a very interesting time in the political history of the country. I had been approached, initially, by Miroslav Tudjman, the son of the President of the country. That was how I ended up in Croatia. So my appointment itself had a political aspect to it. And it was just after the war. You could still feel the aftermath of the conflict in every sense.

Perhaps the clearest example of this, for me, was when we played in Vukovar, a city which had been in the thick of things during the war. We got there and as the plane was landing you could see all the houses, and there wasn't a single one unmarked by shell holes or other gunfire. They were practically destroyed. That really gave me a strong sense of what life was like for these people: they had spent a large portion of their lives in the midst of armed conflicts. I had often thought that even though things were going well for us at the club nobody ever said 'well done' or 'congratu-lations', things like that. I think that was because their preoccupations were centred on other things. If you spend years in a warring environment, how are you going to have the time or the inclination to go round saying 'well done'?

It was a time of regeneration, and when I was there

Croatia was in the middle of a democratic opening up. It wasn't long before President Tudjman died and there were elections which the opposition won – the political opposition to the club president. So the mayor of the city, the club president, everything changed.

But that all happened after I'd gone.

35

Sun, Sea and Sand

Throughout the year I was away in Croatia there was talk about me returning to Japan. And back I went, almost immediately, to Yokohama Marinos – a big club in Japan.

When I was in Japan before, they had been awarded the 2002 World Cup. At least it was Japan until the last minute, then South Korea was included as co-host. For the Japanese it was a big blow not to host the tournament alone. I had been an advocate of the World Cup being held there, not in an official capacity but as a prominent member of the football community, if you like. In December 2000 there was a national squad of Japan and South Korea and I was co-manager against a Rest of the World team. The most famous of their players was Romário, and they were managed by Arrigo Sacchi, who had taken Italy to the World Cup Final in 1994.

I spent two years in Yokohama, a very beautiful city right beside Tokyo, almost joined to it: there's a river between them but you can move between one and the other almost as if they are the same city. Tokyo and Yokohama combined is one of the biggest conurbations in the world. Some forty million people live there. I enjoyed the fact that I could just nip into Tokyo, and that we were in the heart of football country in Japan (most of the football clubs are based in and around Tokyo). I also enjoyed the fact that Yokohama was a successful squad: there are two tournaments in the year in Japan, and Yokohama won the first, the first stage of the J-League.

When I was in Croatia I knew I could go back to Japan, that there remained possibilities for me there, and now I was in Japan I was soon getting offers again from other places. But I didn't really want to delve deeper into talks because I wouldn't leave a club while under contract, especially in Japan. The way the Japanese are, loyalty and commitment are hugely important there. And also I was very grateful to the Japanese, because Japan was where I recovered my confidence as a manager, during those first three years in Shimizu, and then afterwards in Yokohama.

But after two years Saudi Arabia came up as a strong possibility. I'd spent some time in England and Spain in between my commitments in Japan. (I had borrowed a house from a colleague when I was at West Brom and fell in love with the Spanish coast. Now I have a house there. Sun, food, golf, my own language – it's my retreat.) My friends there would insist that I do some TV, some punditry, or get myself out there and do some networking. But I guess I'm too shy, or . . . I don't know what the word is. I just don't find it easy. So all my in-between job stints were incredibly low profile. And I don't have an agent. All my jobs come through an agent who approaches me with an offer. Every deal I make there is at least one agent involved who brings the deal together for all parties (except in Japan: all the clubs I worked at there I was taken to by a businessman called Karai Tadashi who is now a very good friend). The agent who had negotiated the Croatia deal with Miroslav Tudjman was a man called Mladen Petreski, and he suddenly contacted me again with the idea of going to Saudi Arabia.

Money is not a problem in Saudi Arabia. All the clubs, the stadiums, the pitches, they're absolutely tip-top. Amazing. But in a way, that wealth is also what prevents them from taking up the place they could take in world football. Because it's a society in which Saudi people, proper Saudis, don't work. The people who work there are all foreign, ex-pats and so on. Although they are the most important national side in the Gulf region, they are not as good as they should be.

I joined one of the biggest clubs, Al-Ittihad, in Jeddah. The dynamics of the place are such that a lot of factors affect selection to the national squad, for example, which doesn't always reflect who the best players in the country are. It's just how it is there. It was clearly the case, for instance, that if the King or the Prince wanted someone to play they had the final word, at national and club level. I noticed among my own players that they didn't have that anxiety about, and hunger for, representing their homeland the way players from other nations do. They just didn't seem particularly bothered about playing for their country, and for me that had always been the ultimate aim.

At Al-Ittihad we won practically every match we played, and we were top of the league. Then suddenly there was a huge political shift within the club. The club president changed, but the president who had hired me assured me, 'Don't worry, nothing should change for you.' But during my first meeting with the new chairman I had a strong inkling that all was not well. It was pretty clear to me that he wanted to come in and make changes. It wasn't really necessary, if football results were the aim, because we were doing extremely well and we were going to be champions. But I guess this

new man felt that was all the old president's achievement, and he wanted to break away from that.

Every day in the press there were stories of a new
manager coming. And when that starts to happen the
squad immediately experiences a dip in trust and confidence. But we carried on playing and winning. In fact,
by the time I actually left the club we still had not lost a
game.

One day the picture of the new manager appeared in
the paper. It was Oscar, a Brazilian I knew because he
had also worked in Japan. The caption underneath said
something like 'Al-Ittihad's new manager arrives'. That
same day the president called me and said, 'Osvaldo, we
have a problem.' I went in to see him, he opened a door,
and there was Oscar with his assistant.

That had never happened to me before in football,
and it will never happen to me again. You can't wake up
one morning and find another manager in your place!
Oscar was very embarrassed because he didn't know I
didn't know.

The first decision had to be who would manage the
team that night – yes, this all took place on a match day!
– so I said, 'Oscar, let's step into my office, which will
now be yours . . .' As soon as we were alone he
apologized profusely, of course; it was an embarrassing
situation for both of us and he'd really had no idea. We

decided that I would go on the bench, and that it would be my last match.

During the tactical talk that evening, before the match, I told the players. I said I wanted them to go out and play for themselves. In the past I had always defended them. The new president was quite a dictatorial figure. He wanted to fine the players for not saying hello with due reverence, things like that. I always stood up for them, so they liked me a lot, in truth.

During the match, one of our Brazilian players scored and came running up to the bench to celebrate with me. Another goal – the players gathered round me to celebrate again. We scored five times, and on each occasion they all ran up to me on the bench. It was 5–2 at the final whistle. That was my last match.

That's how it is in football.

Life in Saudi was quite interesting. The religious side of things being so closely intertwined with daily life was new to me. In Saudi, religion is incredibly important. It's so hot there, unbearably hot, that we would train at night, and the last prayer of the day would happen during training. So the call to prayer would come from the mosques and my assistant, who was Saudi, would say, 'OK, Osvaldo.' I would then stand around for ten minutes or so while everyone – the players, the team staff, almost every single person there – turned to face Mecca and started praying. Of course I wasn't alone: there were three Brazilians in the team, the stars of the side, and they would stand around with me, speaking incredibly quietly. We couldn't do anything else – touch the ball or anything like that.

If the King came to a game, whenever he arrived, the match stopped; only once he had taken his seat could we continue playing.

I remember one game against a team who had a big, tall central defender. His shorts were too small for him so the referee sent him to get changed on the grounds that his attire was offensive. So he went and got changed, but he was a big guy and the other pair of shorts were still too tight. When he returned the ref said, 'No, still offensive,' and he demanded that the player sit out the game. He forced a substitution! Another guy played instead. It was team selection taken to a whole new level.

I was living in Saudi when the 11 September attacks took place in New York. We heard about it on our way to the airport, due to travel to the capital. Very dramatic moments ensued: there were rumours about the perpetrators having links to Saudi Arabia and much nervousness because no one knew what the US reaction would be. Security was intensified; the tension was palpable. My own eventual departure was unrelated to this: a new chairman took over the club and he got rid of all the foreigners – not just me but all the non-Saudi players in the squad. We all left.

I was on a beach in Spain having left Al-Ittihad when I got a call from Argentina. Racing, one of the oldest and most traditional clubs in the country, were offering me the manager's job.

It was in some ways unthinkable. The manager there was Reinaldo 'Mostaza' Merlo and he had just won the Argentinian championship. I'd thought it impossible that Merlo would leave, but I got this call and apparently he had resigned. Did I want the job? As I said, I was lying on the beach with some friends at the time. I said yes without thinking twice.

My return to Argentina – it was the first time I'd gone back to work there since the World Cup in 1978, nearly a quarter of a century earlier – was incredible. Merlo had made Racing into champions for the first time in thirty-five years. But there had been problems between him and the club management, which is why he'd left. The fans erected a statue in his honour!

In Argentina, clubs are not privately owned. Presidents and directors are voted in by the members of the club. But club administration is quite corrupt, quite inefficient. Racing had become a pioneer in the sense that a private company had taken over the management of the club. It was this company that hired me.

A gigantic club, hoping to make history by modernizing its management, with a beloved, iconic, but now departed manager.

I was back in the eye of the storm.

36

Home from Home

Argentina was in the middle of huge economic chaos. In fact, economically speaking, the country had literally collapsed. Those who could leave were doing so. We went back just as these people were fleeing.

But Racing was something of an island. The opposite of what was going on in the country was happening there. We got paid every month, punctually, European style. At the end of every month everyone's wages were paid straight into the bank. No one ever came to complain they were owed money or anything like that. The installations, the club facilities, the infrastructure, all were perfect. It was a big deal in Argentina, even more so in 2002. Clubs were not used to the way Racing were doing things. It was a very exciting moment in the country's football history.

The political climate in the country was tense,

however. The economic crisis had reached a climax in December 2001, when people took to the streets banging pots and pans, demanding access to their bank accounts which had been frozen. Known as the *cacerolazo*, the debacle that had led to the toppling of the government had taken place, ironically, on the scheduled final day of the football season, when Racing were to be crowned champions. The fixture was moved at the last minute. When I took the Racing job there was nowhere in Argentinian football more tied up with the sense of hope and a new dawn.

As a football man I take all my professional decisions with the sport itself at the forefront of my mind. I had learned in 1978 and 1982 that political circumstances can be adverse, but the game goes on. I think if one were to compare the chaos of 2001/02 with 1978 or 1982 it was less intense, but it's probably up there with them.

For me personally it didn't have a direct impact. The single issue I had to face was that of security (or rather insecurity). We had an incident at the club, when Diego Milito's father was kidnapped. Diego was playing for Racing and his younger brother Gabi was at Independiente, just down the road, and both clubs had been contacted by the kidnappers for ransom money. The father was released unharmed, but the wave of kidnappings which seemed to be replacing petty theft in the streets of Buenos Aires became the number one issue for ordinary people. And if you were a public figure you were obviously more exposed.

On the pitch, stepping into Merlo's shoes was quite something. People said I was carrying his baggage, but I never felt that way, in all honesty. Still, there was clearly a legacy that would be a challenge to live up to.

Every club I've been to as a manager I've tried not to bring with me too many people as staff. But if I can take one person, one very trusted person, I like to do that. Except in Croatia. When I arrived in that country their equivalent of the *Sun*, the main tabloid, published my salary. I was on a very good contract. With what I was earning you could pay I don't know how many salaries of normal working people – and remember, they were just out of a war. After publication the chairman asked me not to hire anyone or bring in any more people, at least for the time being. But in Saudi I'd taken with me Ray Scott, a friend from England. In Japan, of course, Steve Perryman was with me. When Racing came along it seemed obvious to ask an Argentinian friend to join me in my new adventure.

And who better than Ricky Villa?

Another person already working at the club was Emilio Commisso. He was the football coordinator, a man from Córdoba whose younger brother had played with me at Instituto. I knew him well, had known his brother all my life, so the triumvirate of Emilio, Ricky and me was as familiar as I could hope for. The Racing 'kitchen' was complete!

My first year there was nothing short of spectacular. I think one of the moments most people remember is when the first goal was scored under my management and I instinctively jumped up and shouted '*Yes!*' – in English. From then on I became 'El Inglés'. And it makes me laugh, too, to recall the way I often let slip a 'C'mon!' to encourage my players. I have yet to issue the warning 'Man on!' to one of my players in a Spanish-speaking country, but I'm sure it could happen.

We played in South America's premier club competition, the Copa Libertadores. Racing had become World Club champions in 1967 after winning the Libertadores, beating Celtic, so this was even more of a meaningful competition for the club. We got through the first stage but didn't have a squad sufficiently big to endure both the domestic league and the Libertadores. The issue soon became which one we would sacrifice. I recall a meeting with the managing company to discuss which trophy we should go for. But how could we sacrifice a tournament, or a cup? It was unthinkable. We were top of the league, we couldn't suddenly start with a reserve side. And the same applied to the Libertadores.

We continued to fight on both fronts and started to suffer the consequences of trying to bite off more than we could chew. In the league Carlos Bianchi's Boca beat us at home. Well, it can happen. Then, in the Libertadores, we had to play at home against a Colombian side and both legs of the match ended in a draw, so the game went to penalties. We were knocked out of the competition, without having lost a single match.

After that game I decided to leave, partly because it wasn't long to the end of the league season and I knew the club was going to start deteriorating (which is actually what happened). But mostly because I felt that was it. I had less than a month left on my contract. My time was up.

As a manager you have a timespan, I think. A shelf life. You have to make the most of that moment, the time you spend there, but when you sense that time has come to an end, that's it. For example, I knew three or four players would leave the club, probably the most important ones – in fact Diego Milito and Mariano Gonzalez did both leave for Europe at the end of the season – and that a whole new team would have to be built. So I resigned. I stepped aside.

* * *

Not long after I left Argentina, my old friend Karai, who was working with Tokyo Verdy in Japan, offered me the manager's job at the club. Japan was still keeping track of my whereabouts and circumstances. There has always been interest in me from that country. They were very tuned in to what I was doing.

Tokyo Verdy is owned by NTV, one of the big Japanese television networks. It was a very important club, one of the founders of the J-League, and for a long time it had dominated the league. But when I arrived they were fighting relegation.

We picked up, and with five fixtures to go we were closing in on the top. We actually won the Emperor's Cup – the Japanese equivalent of the FA Cup – which was a pending assignment for me, high up on my to-do list. I had won the league with Yokohama and the Nabisco Cup (the League Cup) with Shimizu, but I'd never won the Emperor's Cup. When I did so with Tokyo Verdy I became the only manager ever to win all three trophies.

The Emperor's Cup, like the FA Cup, is very traditional. The knockout phase of the tournament culminates in December, and the final is always played on 1 January. The Japanese are very well organized, so we'd play a game at whatever stage of the competition and all the foreigners would have plane tickets booked for the next day, so if you lost you were off, on holiday, back home, wherever, until the beginning of the next season in early February. Silvia had flown home already and every match I was thinking I might be with her the next day, but we went through every time. I spent my first Christmas in Japan, which was interesting. It is marked as a bank holiday but exists only commercially; it's totally devoid of religion. And because the Emperor's Cup Final is on 1 January, if you make it to the final New Year's Eve is a pre-match night!

I had come a long way from the very first Christmas we'd spent in England, which had also been hard. We were used to family and a break from football; the Boxing Day match, for example, was a complete novelty for us. Now I was picking up the Emperor's Cup in Japan on New Year's Day!

The following season wasn't so good, maybe because my expectations were too high after winning the cup. We had a couple of key players injured, and the squad was short. That was it, I felt.

It's very tough to stay at the top in football. I admire Alex Ferguson so much. Because to remain there . . . for how long? How long has he been there? Twenty years? More! It's a spectacular achievement.

This is something I've grown to understand as I've

got older. It's bound up with the importance of change, by which I mean what I've explained before – adaptability. If you've won the World Cup, for example, the temptation *not* to change is huge. I think this happened to Menotti in 1978, for example. He didn't change enough for 1982. You can have top players, all the best facilities and trimmings, but without change you'll stagnate.

When we won the Emperor's Cup I thought no change was needed, but it was. I left things as they were. If I could do it all over again I would implement more changes at Tokyo Verdy, in every way. End of one season. Full stop. New season, new everything. Of course you must balance this with a measure of continuity, which is what Ferguson gets right. And he makes brave changes. Look at how he handled Beckham. Not many managers would be able to do that. Beckham was one of the most important, high-profile players in his team, they were champions, yet Ferguson recognized the need for change. He brought in Ronaldo, who was not exactly unknown but still a prospect. You need to be confident to do something like that.

Without change a team risks becoming complacent, too full of the thought that 'everything's OK, so why change?' That is dangerous. Why change? Because the other teams have changed . . . circumstances have changed . . . everything else has changed. Nothing lasts for ever. And that's maybe why it's so difficult to repeat success – to win the World Cup twice in a row, for instance. And it's the same for every national championship and cup competition.

It's much harder to stay at the top than to get there.

37

War and Faith

I left Tottenham at the end of 1994 feeling suffocated by a chairman v. manager wrangle that had turned incredibly sour. It was a turning point in the way the football industry operated, the beginning of TV money and cross-industry marriages. It started me off on a globe-trotting adventure which allowed me to see how football operates in all sorts of places. In Mexico the president of Chivas was a businessman with links to the petrol industry. In Japan the clubs are owned by big-brand companies – Mitsubishi, Nissan, Toyota – and the companies designate club presidents as corporate staff, employees of the company whose job it is to run the club. In Argentina clubs are 'owned' by the fans, and run by men of football who are 'voted' into power.

In Israel I went to Beitar Jerusalem, one of the four big clubs in the country, owned by Arkadi Gaydamak, a

Russian Jewish billionaire on a par with Roman Abramovich. The year I was there, 2006, Gaydamak was named 'man of the year' in Israel. But there were also international arrest warrants with his name on them, issued in France. He had been involved, using his business connections, in the release of two French soldiers kidnapped in Bosnia, for which he was given the Légion d'Honneur, one of the highest accolades in France. But he had been involved in alleged tax evasion and illegal arms dealing in Angola too – a scandal in which President Mitterrand's son had also been implicated – and that resulted in the arrest warrants. In England his connections came under scrutiny as well, mainly because his son Alexander owned Portsmouth.

But however a club's structures operate, and whoever sits at the top of the board table, the manager's task is always the same: it's the crucial link between president, staff and players. In my opinion, the most important part, the absolute top of the pyramid, are the players. Without them you're going nowhere. Everything else – the board, the media, and the press has a huge role – is secondary. The task is huge, because the manager has to constantly strike the balance. He has to keep on top of the relationship with the players first and foremost, but he must also be the main liaison with the chairman, the directors, the administrative staff, the fans . . . And all the time the football has to remain the main focus. As I've said before, it's all a matter of playing and deciding how to play. And the results have to support the ideology.

My first meeting with Gaydamak was at his house, a spectacular palace in Caesarea overlooking the sea, surrounded by incredibly tight security. It seemed to me I had travelled a long way from that first visit to Alan Sugar's house in the outer suburbs of London. The meeting was supposedly a feeler before my appointment was confirmed, but the first thing I'd been shown when I flew into Israel was a photograph in the papers of the Israeli Prime Minister, Gaydamak and the club chairman Vladimir Shklar at Vladimir's daughter's wedding. The paper reported that the Prime Minister had been told of my appointment. And the Prime Minister was a Beitar supporter. I took that to mean I had the job!

We knocked on the door and a very tall guy in a long black coat opened it and showed us in. I was with Vladimir and Ronny Rosenthal, who was working as a football agent and had brokered the deal. The first thing Gaydamak told me was this: 'I don't like football. Eleven men running after a ball, I don't see the point.' OK, I thought, I'm dealing with Jorge Luis Borges here. And then, after a few exchanges, he suddenly said, 'I don't think you're the man for this job.' This meeting was going from bad to worse. He said I was too much of a gentleman, too polite ... and then he asked me if I knew any Jewish people. I told him I had some Jewish friends, that Tottenham has strong links with the Jewish community, and he remarked 'Israeli Jews are very different, you know.'

'OK, I'd like you to sign for three years,' he then said.

In fact I signed for one year with a two-year option to renew.

My first game – the first match of the league campaign, in August 2006 – was a baptism of fire, against Maccabi Tel Aviv. We played them at their home ground and beat them, and Beitar hadn't done that for I don't know how many years . . . maybe twenty. And we beat them 2–1.

We'd played a very important match before that, against Dinamo Bucharest of Romania, to decide who would go on to play in the UEFA Cup. It was a home and away two-legged match but, because of the war situation, European clubs weren't coming to Israel so for our home match we played in Bulgaria. We drew this 'home' tie but lost the away leg, and we were out of the competition.

But in the domestic league we were going up. The club was like the Boca of Israel. The pressure was

monstrous, permanently. It was so intense. Overwhelming. After our historic win at Maccabi, a very
difficult match, our second match was against Hapoel
Tel Aviv, another big club, at home. We had a player sent
off thirty minutes into the match, we went a goal
behind, then with ten minutes to go we scored twice
and won. The stadium went crazy.

In the space of a few days we'd defeated two of our
main competitors. We were top of the league, but I kept
feeling this pressure from all quarters and I remember
sensing, around the time when we lost one match, that
although we were still first in the league the end was
nigh. Emilio Commisso had come with me to Israel as
my assistant, and I can recall saying to him, 'Hmm, it's
not looking good.'

A couple of weeks before I was sacked Gaydamak
held a big party to celebrate the Jewish New Year in a
really fancy restaurant on the outskirts of Jerusalem,
overlooking the hills. It was a superb place. He invited
everyone at the club and gave them all, absolutely every
single person, a present: Vladimir, me, all the players, all
the kitmen, everybody. I was sitting at a table with
Silvia, Commisso and his wife, Vladimir, Gaydamak
himself and one of his sons. When the meal was over he
said to me, 'Osvaldo, congratulations, you're doing a
great job.'

Fifteen days later, bye-bye.

There were some incredible characters at that club. Abraham was one. He was in his mid-sixties and he was the coordinator of the team's affairs. We had training every day and he organized everything: the trips, the meals, everything. He was Mr Beitar Jerusalem. He'd been at the club for thirty years and had held every post from kitman to president, from masseur to coach. He made a bit of a blooper just before our UEFA Cup match against Dinamo Bucharest, though. The club had just signed two players and he'd thought they could be presented to UEFA up to twenty-four hours before the match to have their names included in the squad list. But it wasn't twenty-four hours, it was forty-eight – a huge mistake, because it meant neither player was able to play, in an important match. Vladimir and another character wanted to sack him immediately. But they didn't.

One time, after a match we'd won, Vladimir said we should all go out to dinner to celebrate. It had been an international fixture week and we had several players who'd also played for Israel. One of them came up to me and said, 'Osvaldo, we've been on international duty and haven't seen our families for days. We'd like to go home.' So I said, of course. Abraham, who'd seen this exchange, had a real go at the player. He spoke in

Hebrew but he was clearly angry and I could tell he was being severe. He seemed to be insisting that it was compulsory to go to this dinner, which was meant to be a club celebration. I stepped in and put my foot down. 'There is no dinner!' I shouted. 'Everybody home! That's it!' Quite uncharacteristic for me, but I felt compelled.

Not long after that Vladimir sacked him. Abraham was a symbol of the old school at the club, and Vladimir was a Russian appointed by the new ownership. There were some slightly annoying things about Abraham, but I respected him a lot for many reasons, but mainly for one: the players genuinely liked him. They had heartfelt appreciation for him. He was, after all, Mr Beitar Jerusalem, a legend at the club.

Once, when years and years earlier he had been manager and Beitar won the title, Abraham was so ecstatic that he jolted up from the bench and banged his head on the roof of the dugout. He was knocked unconscious and had to be carried away on a stretcher. He was a total character, Abraham.

But when he got sacked by Vladimir a story went round suggesting it was because of the altercation he and I had had. It was clear to me that the Russians wanted to get him out of the way so I went to see him and told him I had absolutely nothing to do with this, no way had I demanded his resignation, I had enough on my plate. 'I know, I know,' he said.

Then came a popular uprising involving the papers, the fans and the Prime Minister. How can there be a Beitar without Abraham? they asked. He was reinstated.

As a life experience, my time at Beitar was unique, and not just in a professional sense. Jerusalem is a beautiful city. Israel is stunning. We used to go a lot to the Dead Sea and walk on the salty water. So beautiful. And it was summer so we went to some amazing beaches in the north of Israel. It's a small country so you can get to the coast within the hour; everything's near. And of course Jerusalem's historic old city made our stay there incredibly interesting.

We soon got used to the religious aspect of daily life. In Jerusalem especially everything closes on the Sabbath. The first time we got stuck unprepared, but after that we understood. One can say all sorts of things about Judaism, Israel, Jerusalem even, but until you live there you can't really understand what it's like. In Jerusalem, daily life is governed by religion. In Tel Aviv it's almost the opposite. Tel Aviv is like Buenos Aires.

Beitar was, historically, a club of the most orthodox, rabidly anti-Arab sectors of this very sectarian world. Some Israeli clubs have Arab or Muslim players. In Beitar we had our quota of foreign players, but only one

Muslim – from Africa – at one point. He was a young boy, nineteen years old, and he was a very good player. But the fans spoke out furiously against his inclusion in the team. I was insulted for playing a Muslim! And we were such a prestigious team that wherever we played the majority of fans were ours. I hadn't even known he was a Muslim originally; the only thing I was interested in was how good he was with a ball at his feet. And he was really good. But every time he got a touch of the ball in matches the terraces turned nasty. I don't like to succumb to pressure from anybody when it comes to selecting my team, but this lad was young and the issues underlying the vitriol ran too deep. I suggested we find him another club, anywhere else, where he could develop his promising attributes and turn into a great player. At Beitar it was going to be impossible. We did find him another club.

Israel combined the war-torn experiences of Croatia with the profound religiosity of Saudi Arabia. The intensity of the beliefs held by all sides, who have existed for decades in a permanent state of war, charges everything, permeates everything. A lot of the players in our squad were also soldiers; they came to training in military uniform! Israel invaded Lebanon while I was there and the stress and tension affected us all. We could no longer play international matches at home, and several players we had intended to buy were unable to join the club – it became incredibly difficult to function. I had replaced former French international Luis Fernández at Beitar, and I'd heard that every morning he used to have all the newspapers translated because he had become so embroiled in needing to understand what was being said, about him, about the club, about the internal strife. He'd become obsessed with this.

I'd decided not to know the details. I feared I might go crazy if I was constantly aware of all the spite. My interest was on the pitch, and there I did not fail.

38

Dust to Dust

I started my professional career in football for real in 1975 at Huracán in Buenos Aires. I arrived just after Carlos Babington, a legendary player for the club, left. Babington had played in the 1974 World Cup and had now gone off to play club football in West Germany. He was a big name in Argentinian football. His nickname, ironically, was El Inglés (the Englishman).

By 2007 Babington had won the elections and become president of Huracán. He offered me the job of manager. It wasn't as easy a decision for me as Racing had been, but the appeal was strong nevertheless. Returning to my first big club, although not quite on the same level as managing Tottenham, was tempting. I played at Tottenham for a decade, at Huracán for only three years, and during the third of those I'd been on international duty for months. But it was still, of course, a return. And in the end I didn't turn it down.

When I first arrived the players didn't know very much about me – in Argentina I'm someone who comes from England! Who is El Inglés? they were probably wondering. I was replacing 'El Turco' Mohamed, another symbolic man for the club. The players' confidence was very low: they were convinced that without El Turco they were going to get relegated, because his departure had been a big blow for them.

They might not have known who I was but we formed a strong bond very quickly. I soon found my team among the squad, and our football campaign went very well. But I had some problems with Babington, which got nasty. I don't think I want to dwell on what happened, but basically the way the club was running its business affairs was shoddy. Everything I don't like about football and the industry.

I ended up fighting with Babington through the press. The players weren't being paid. In fact, when I was appointed I had had to fund my trip to Argentina and pay for a stay in a hotel. This was a ludicrous situation for a big club. There were numerous other small details that were all wrong.

I don't know if Babington felt threatened by me, if there was an element of personal competition or jealousy, or what. Certainly the players were fascinated by my experiences, asking a lot about what it was like to win the World Cup – as opposed to just playing in it – about my experiences in England and Tottenham's achievements at club level, winning European trophies etc. I think I could happily have stayed at Huracán. The football results were on my side – we beat River Plate, we beat Newell's, and the last game of the season we beat Vélez – the players were absolutely on my side, we were coming up for the Christmas break – I could have a holiday, distance myself a bit, have a breather, then go back – but the problems made me decide to quit. I just knew I didn't want to be at the club under those circumstances.

Managing in Argentina can be tough. There are a lot of conflicts, a lot of political tensions, a lot of problems. I guess the experience of managing Huracán proved, as if proof were necessary, that there can be no return to good old days.

Throughout my career I have followed football both in Argentina and in England with a keen interest. This interest has been keenest with regard to the clubs I've been involved with, of course, and the most special place in my heart is reserved for Tottenham. I arrived there over thirty years ago thinking, 'Three years and I'm out of football.' But I never left.

Argentina is my birthplace, my country, my football nationality for sure. In fact I never got British citizenship or a British passport, purely because I felt that having won the World Cup with Argentina it would be wrong to 'be' a different nationality, that I should retain my Argentinian-ness, if I can put it like that. Silvia has a British passport, as do my boys, but I don't.

But Argentina is the past. My father has died now, my mother is old. Of course Córdoba is home in a way that nowhere else can ever be, and I own some land there and go back every year – have done every year since I moved away. But England is the future. It is the land of my grandchildren. I think the natural cycle of life is to follow one's children, and mine and theirs are in England.

Will I ever return to Argentina for more than a holiday? Who knows? It's always the question, and one, I suspect, that can only be answered as the story unfolds. Without doubt I would for a good management job. Much in the same way that I would go anywhere.

Management is the only way to stay in football, and football is my life. I know that most of my former teammates, from every club and every country, probably feel the same way. Whatever any one of them is doing now, I know they spend their whole time thinking about football.

It's very hard for us to lead a quiet life, a calm life away from football. We need that adrenalin. And that's why if you asked me now 'What are you dying to do?' I'd answer, 'Manage.' That's why I went to Huracán.

In an ideal world where I could choose the place, it would be England. It's the best country in the world to work in. The football industry has transformed into a world leader. The football game is played as it should be.

And if you asked me 'What is your dream, your real dream?', well, apart from managing a national side in a World Cup, it's simple: I would give anything to be able to play one more match. I don't mean a kickabout with some mates, I mean a real proper football match.

Just to walk into the dressing room, all the kit laid out, the new socks, the boots . . . everything ready.

Just to do a little run on the spot, a bit of jumping to warm up, then to walk out of the tunnel on to the turf of a real stadium.

Just to hear the roar of the crowd and let my mind compute all the emotions and thoughts and strategies simultaneously: my loved ones, my loyalties, my fitness, and above all, who is going to be marking me?

Just to hear the whistle blow, and for the game to start.

Acknowledgements

In the writing of this book I would like to thank Marcela Mora y Araujo for putting my thoughts into words. Thanks to David Luxton for putting the deal together with Transworld Publishers, to Giles Elliott for his editing skills and enthusiasm for all things Latin American, to Daniel Balado, and to all the Transworld team, including Phil Lord and Kate Tolley.

Football has been my life, and has given me the opportunity to travel, see the world and meet all sorts of people. I am grateful to the game for this. I have been involved with many charities – Special Olympics, Sparks, The Willow Foundation of Megs and Bob Wilson, the Bobby Moore Foundation among others – an experience which has enriched me much more than I can hope to have contributed to their cause.

So many people have been a part of my many jobs at

every stage of my life that it is impossible to name them all. But I do want to express heartfelt gratitude to the staff – the kitmen, the physiotherapists, the medical staff, the management – at all the clubs I have been involved in, particularly those of Tottenham Hotspur. A very special thanks to the fans too, and last but very much not least to all the players: the heart and soul of the game.

Picture Acknowledgements

Index